Losing Eyesight, But Gaining Vision

by

Fred Don Cullens

Published in the United States of America

Cullens, Fred Don - 1941

ISBN 13 – 978-1491039366

ISBN 10 - 1491039361

Tonya Holmes Shook, Publishing Coordinator

Table of Contents

Foreword

And we know that all things work together for good to them that love God, to them who are the called according to his purpose. (Romans 8:28)

Fred Don certainly illustrates this Biblical truth. He is losing his eyesight, yet sees how God has used this tragic even to bless and enlighten him. Here is a photo of Fred and I a few years back at our 50th high school reunion.

E. Norbert Smith, Ph.D. and Fred Don Cullens.

Fred Don and I were in the same class and became good friends in high school. His family owned the local bakery where my mother eventually worked. He attended the local Assembly of God church and I was a Baptist. We had many heated discussions about the gifts of the Holy Spirit, speaking in tongues and many other denominational differences we had experienced. Years later I realized he was correct and I was wrong on several of these issues. Sadly, as often happens with high school friends we went our separate ways and lost contact after our graduation in 1959. Luckily we re-connected at our 50th high school reunion in 2009 and have stayed in touch.

It seems he had a difficult time deciding what he wanted to do when he "got big" and has done an impressive variety of things in his life as you will see in this book. Like most of us, his life has had many bumps along the way and a few of them he place there himself.

Norbert Smith
Fred Don's lifelong friend.

Losing eyesight, but gaining vision

Introduction

How fast time flies! When we are young, the passage of time seems to be dragging. We often yearn for the swift acquisition of: the first date, high school graduation, first car, the first job…the list is endless. But we are pushing forward and to "success".

The reality of time slipping faster than we realize is a growing awareness as we push toward the higher number of years…The age of 40 is a "wake up call" for many and before we know it, we are looking back at our life as we push the retirement years. We never know what life will hand us as we reach the "sundown" years. The human spirit is often stronger than we first believe. It has been said that "if life gives you lemons….make lemonade". What if you don't like lemonade? Perhaps you can acquire a taste or sell it?

The purpose of this book is to give an honest and frank expression of a personal experience. It will be a true story based on my personal interaction with the "lemons" of life. It is my hope that some of my conclusions will give the reader a moment of "ah" or allow an acceptance without guilt feelings and emotions.

My full name is Fred Don Cullens and I am 70 years old at the time of writing this first draft of my memoir. I confess that I am surprised that I am actually that old. My backward look seems to be colored by amazement that time has passed so quickly. I look back with a sense of personal awe over the road I have traveled. I can now see the rocky pathway, the times of success and times of wrong choices with the results. It never entered my mind at any time that I would end my life "walking in shadows". I am blind! I must be more accurate; I am "legally blind". As discovered about 10 years ago after cataract surgery. The eye disease *retinitis pigmentosa* was confirmed by the eye specialist and my field of vision was less than 20 degrees. I met the legal definition of statuary blindness as defined by the Social Security Disability Program. This was the beginning of my walk in darkness.

It is often that I cannot sleep. I have learned to just get up and "do" something. One of my pastimes is to make coffee coasters out of plastic canvass. I give them away when I encounter people. It makes the time go faster and I can listen to a book or music while being creative. I have discovered that I spend more time "living" in my mind. Since I can no longer see very well, I spend much time in thought and reliving past events. This may not be unusual as we grow old. I don't know, but it brings me some pleasure and sometimes sadness.

I have had a good life, not a perfect life, not a life without pain and heartache and certainly not with riches; but it has been a good one. God has a plan for each of us, and if we understand Him, He actually has more than just one. We are free agents and can make choices. We can choose to avoid God's plan and go our own way. He is then able to make our rebellion to "work together for good". I look back and accept that I side stepped God's perfect will for me; but discovered His permissive will and He covered me anyway. Moses retained the favor of God after Moses disobeyed and HIT the rock for water, rather than SPEAKING to it, but he was denied the opportunity to enter the "Promised Land" due to his disobedience. I have come to the conclusion that we are forgiven by God but still have to deal with the harvest and the results of our actions.

I have enjoyed many roles in my life. I started a public preaching ministry at age 8 with a definite "call to the ministry". I have been the pastor of three Assembly of God Churches, part of the Hartford's Middle Management Training force, in Hartford, Connecticut, worked as social worker for Cheyenne County Welfare Office, in Sidney, Nebraska, taught high school English and Speech in Los Fresnos, Texas, traveled for over 5 years as a Financial Planner/Stockbroker conducting day long seminars in a different major city each day, was the administrator of 12 nursing homes, 1 hospital located in 11 Texas cities, for four years I worked as a full-time substitute teacher in Odessa, Texas, teaching all 12 grades as well an pre-school and I had over 9 years as a Social Security Disability Specialist. I enjoyed each function and attained a level of satisfaction in each. This employment trip produced over 90 awards, certificates and framed "brag sheets" to hang on my wall. I added to my education until I had a total of 8 degrees, certificates or completion awards. These covered Education, Theology, Sociology/Psychology and Business Management. I had earned and honorary doctorates to dress up my office walls. I enjoyed good work and professional life but it had a steep price.

I learned the hard lesson that God is not found inside ANY one church nor does he favor any church label. The power of the Bible has been so weakened by our "religion" that even God would not claim ownership to what we try to force people to believe. My last experience with the "organized" church forced me to see and feel the wrath of the corruption in church politics. This pushed me into all of the "tent-making" jobs mentioned. I understand Paul the tent-maker very well.

I started this section at 4 a.m. on Friday morning. Forgive me as I do not intend to bore you with too much detail and I understand it is possible to provide "too much information".

I had nothing to blame for my eye problem. It was a birth defect produced by a gene defect. Who can you blame? The first impact was a rock hard assault on my total being. I was given amazing support and practical help by the Commission for the Blind in Odessa, Texas. My vision was and remains greatly affected by the glare of any light and the sun. I was given "white cane" training and was considered for a seeing-eye dog. This was vetoed as I had too much vision remaining and I would not totally depend on a guide dog. The theory was that I would "over-ride" the guide dog by using what vision I had. I was not all that hindered in my abilities when in-doors with proper lighting. I have lived alone for over 22 years and have taken care of myself effectively.

The past two years my vision has faded. Circumstances forced me to retire and face my "golden years" a bit earlier than expected. I still live alone and with the help of "Meals-on-Wheels" and a small group of friends, I am still able to maintain my ability to live alone. That brings you up to date with a minimum of unnecessary details.

Purpose of This Little Book

This brings me to the purpose of this writing. There is no limit to book writing and every person has a story to tell. I am no different. It may be somewhat presumptive to think my story has benefit for the reader; however, the freedom to express personal opinions and feelings is a cornerstone of our lifestyle.

I am a man of faith! I make no apology for that fact. I am not a man of a "church". My spiritual walk may be the subject of another book, but let me tell you that I am an ordained clergyman with a history of preaching, leading churches as well as a TV, radio and prison ministry. That was my childhood anchor and still shapes my thought patterns. I left the formal church and discovered the reality of the "spiritual church" as opposed to the political church. This gave me a deeper personal freedom as I was able to scrape away the "mandatory" guilt required by "man-made" religion. I am spiritual, but not religious.

We behave the way we do based on what we believe. This truth was understood as I studied to become a "Licensed Belief Therapist". It becomes necessary to examine our belief system in order to explain our behavior. Guilt feeds feelings of being inferior can hide our true "Christ in you…the hope of glory."

The fact of blindness hammered at my personal image. I will honestly tell you that when I was told by the doctor, whose bedside manner was somewhat crisp, that I needed to forget going back to work…but apply for disability as I was going blind; I was stunned! What a thunderbolt out of the blue! I have perfect health. I do not take a single pill for any reason. I only take some herbs.   I   have   no   health   or   medical expenses…none….and now I am going blind!

It would be nice to be able to tell you that as a good Christian I was able to be gracious and trusting with the truth that "God was in control". I would like to tell you that….but it would not be an honest report. Oh yes, we are told that we "shouldn't" have certain feelings. Feelings and emotions are neither good nor bad, they just are. The belief structure that promotes the denial of feelings and emotions is probably a leading cause for mental and emotional problems in our world. Christ does not require that we become "liars" in order to absorb His teachings.

I went home after the flat statement by the doctor and wept for over two weeks. I wept over the loss of vision, the death of my Father, the loss of my marriage, the loss of my work ability, the loss of mother dying in a nursing home as a "vegetable." I cried until one morning I had no more tears and stopped. This was the release of a lifetime of trying to sugarcoat the rocks of life with spiritual motto and little gospel ditties. You know them;

the family that prays together, stays together….Christians never get angry….etc. These sayings look nice hanging on the wall…but they are not realistic in living life. I had preached this lifestyle…and discovered the pitfall.

Please understand, I do believe in the overall awareness and control of God…but realize that the roadmap to that awareness is a painful walk in truth…not just "Pollyanna" mottos. The process of adjusting lifestyle to the limitations provided by reality can be embraced or bitterly refused. The choice will determine the shaping of your lifestyle, world and the world's response to you.

I am living each day with the awareness that my vision is growing dimmer. I have accepted the declining ability to cook my own meals. This is painful as I love to cook…but when you can no longer see the stove controls, or see what is in the fridge, you are walking a path of danger by continued denial. Meals-on-Wheels has been my salvation. I can still make my breakfast and supper with simple cooking, which may or may not slowly vanish. My great fear was how to continue to live and take care of myself.

It never crossed my mind that I would reach the "golden years" alone and blind. But choices always dictate outcome. I can't blame God, my mother or the United Nations for decisions that led to the death of family and marriage. Like it or not, we make our choices.   Yes, God forgives mistakes and stupid actions…but seldom is the harvest of seeds planted totally destroyed. I am forgiven, but the aftermath follows. This principle of life is true, "We reap what we sow; like it or not.

I have good days and bad days…I am aware of the wonderful blessings of what I have and often weep with appreciation and gratitude. Yet I have days when I am sad, angry depressed and grief-stricken. How does one accept harsh and painful life issues? This becomes a matter of choice….sometimes I make good choices and sometimes I make mistakes. Neither of these changes the situation and yet they can make all the difference in the world. It is a mind-set. Learn what you can from life and allow the cost of life's learning to be paid and move on. We often hear," just get over it". This is a senseless and thoughtless expression that does not embrace the real process of absorbing life. I have learned a few lessons that I want to pass on to you, the reader, in the hope it might be of some value to you and help justify your purchase of my book. These lessons of necessity come from my experience with blindness, but I feel they can transfer to other limiting conditions.

A. People with limitations

Some people are uncomfortable around people who have limitations. One of my first stepping stones was the issue of using my white cane. I had mixed feelings about "looking" blind. I quickly learned that I needed the cane more to alert others about my awkward behavior when I bumped into someone at a large department store. He was angry and yelled at me to watch where I was going. Frankly, he frightened me. I decided that I could accept people thinking I was blind, rather than thinking of me as a bumbling idiot.   I then made a compromise by using my white support cane rather than the long straight cane of the blind.

I was still using the airlines for my work at this point. The professionals at the airport were wonderful and helpful, but I quickly experienced the avoidance of many people. I observed that many people do not know how to act or respond to a person with "limitations". I have always been a very social person and quickly learned that it was my job to make people comfortable and not the reverse. This underscores a simple truth. "If a person wants friends…he must first show himself friendly." Here is a proverb lesson I learned. People have a short attention span to listen to your problems. They were interested in learning about *retinitis pigmentosa* as I explained it, but not for a lengthy conversation. The lesson: I have to offer more energy toward being friendly…rather than complain about the "coldness" or "aloofness" of others.

B. Preconceived prejudices

I think the most profound lesson I am learning is about our preconceived ideas and prejudices about life and people. The fact is simple…as you lose vision…you can no longer depend on your past concepts and prejudices to relate to people. My vision is dim and I can no longer judge you based on these past guidelines. We judge people based on how they look, what they are wearing, how they look at us and other visual cues. Well, guess what? When you can't see these clues, you can't judge or measure people based on your past conditioned responses. I can't tell if you are wearing a Rolex or a Timex, the size of your diamond is a non-issue, if you are wearing high fashion clothes or bargain basement is no longer important to me. My bridge to you must be built on hearing you and listening to what you say, not how you look. I find this refreshing as I am learning to listen to people and not just look at them. I wonder if we used this measure earlier in life if we would have a richer experience. We would avoid the problems of race, gender or educational prejudice. That would be good.

C. Learning to wait

Patience has never been my strong suite. "I want it now". My blindness had taught me that I am no longer able to do things based on "my" time schedule. I am dependent on others and my perceived emergency may or may not be viewed in the same way by them. I have to wait on someone else for any activity such as food shopping, going out to eat, taking a package to mail or going to any social event. Waiting is a learned grace. My choice is to learn patience and graceful understanding of the time pressure of others, or I can be grumpy, crabby and sour. The latter will reduce my ability to do things! The real value of learning to wait…is to keep my blood pressure normal and to learn to prioritize my needs. Learning to know all that you need each trip to the store is vital. I can no longer just jump in the car and run to the store, nor can I expect my friends to drop what they are doing for my whims. Planning becomes an important virtue. Learning to be truly thankful and expressing the same is another important grace of living I have learned.

D. Simple is better

Why do you keep it?   My world has become simple and uncluttered. I wonder why it took blindness for me to truly appreciate the simple lifestyle. I am so thankful that I had a mother who taught me to be organized and put things back where they belonged. It is easy for me to live the disciple of organization. My sense of touch is gaining importance and my memory helps me continue to do certain tasks. The arrangement of furniture must be maintained. No coffee table in the center of the living room. I have cut back on the furniture to allow for easier mobility. My kitchen is carefully laid out so I can find what I need. Food must always be placed in the same place. I am slowly losing the ability to read what is written on the can so the peas, corn and other food items. I have learned to always put certain foods in the same place; otherwise I will play "surprise, surprise" for meals based on opening a can! This can be funny…but not always welcome.

The matter of clothing, both handing and in the drawer requires some discipline. I am discovering my reduction in color recognition. I have to be extremely careful to keep clothes together than need to be together. I also have discovered the liberty of having fewer clothes to deal with. I am amazed and ashamed of how much money I have wasted during my "clothes hog" days. Why we feel we need so much excess? Oh, I know we claim we need it for business, but looking back I now see it as pride and trying to keep up with our consumer culture. I have given away boxes of clothes, kitchen stuff and stuff that we just put in a box, on a shelf and never use. Clean out and give it to someone who can use it. I have discovered simple and uncluttered is a peaceful way to live. I could have a better retirement income if I had learned this lesson many years ago.

E. The falling away of material value

I have always been a collector. I was a pack rat. I had lots of "stuff". Some stuff never got unpacked, most was never used…but I had stuff. We all need stuff, right? This was a reflection of who I was. I could impress visitors! If you needed one of an item, I had two and more was better…right? This became my replacement for love, marriage and someone to care about me. No, I am not whining, just stating the facts. I was a very good American consumer, spending all I had without too much concern for saving money. We are not a saving people, we are a spending people. We use things to give us identity, to build our self-esteem…etc. I now see all that as baloney. My lack of vision does restrict the usage of many things…it is hard to explain, but even walking is complicated by my lack of vision. Please understand, my conclusions are not based on "sour grapes" although, I have had my times of grief, anger and depression over my loss of vision.

The other side of the coin is that the losses are offset by the positive lessons we can learn, if we chose to learn them. I have discovered the absolute thrill and joy and giving stuff away to others. As Jesus said, ***It is more blessed to give than to receive.*** (Acts 20:35) This is not the American way…but it is the spiritual way. As I am unable to see well enough to use various items, I have embraced the delight of giving it to someone who can. I have always been a generous person and that would be confirmed by anyone who knows me, but my sense of pleasure in giving is greater indeed! You don't have to be blind to learn this lesson. To be honest, I do miss the enjoyment of pictures on the wall, the various whatnots that I delighted in and all the various advantages of sight. I want this book to be honest...not just a Christian bubble, but I am learning that the ability of turning loose of the past and the recognition of when something has out-lived its' purpose carries a sense of inner contentment. Yes, I still have tears over my loss, but more and more my tears are from gratitude and not despair. I know despair and I will talk about that later.

F. Why are you crying?

Learn when it is appropriate to do so. I have explained that I am a man of faith….but I am also a man of tears. I realize that it isn't macho for a man to cry, however tears are real. If men were allowed, as boys, to embrace that side of their nature, the level of high blood pressure and other stress related diseases among men might reduce. Yes, I sometimes cry. I have explained my two weeks of solid tears after my blind sentence.

The past 10 years have allowed me to examine my tears, my moods and my reactions and I have reached the following personal conclusion. I do not claim they represent any basis in science or medicine, nor do I offer them as other than my own attempt to keep my life positive. But for me, it works and it can't hurt for you to consider it. When I had my crying spell at first, I somehow realized that I was crying for more than the blindness. It came to me that I was grieving for many losses in my life.

To give you more accurate background, as I traveled my road into the shadows I found myself sleeping a great deal…sometimes 20 hours out of 24. I decided that I did not meet the definition of Clinical Depression as my mood did not keep me from my self-care; I have always been neat, wash dishes immediately, made my bed and put stuff away. So my excess sleeping was not making my world a mess. Due to my situation of returning Midland, Texas, after 4 years working in Laredo, Texas, I did not have many friends. I really only had about 5 who were close to me and of those only three were able to make trips to visit me. They had their own lives to live. But they were my support line and my forever friends…my adopted family.

Some days I would become very sad, depressed and often had thoughts of dying and yes I even thought of suicide. My life seemed to have no purpose; no meaning and I had no one at the end of the day with whom I could share. As I have explained I have excellent health…however I have taken St. John's Wart for over 30 years as a mood helper. A few times I would stop and would notice my down moods becoming more apparent. I would cry and feel so alone.

I am not sure when I started to understand that there was more I could do to help myself. One of my problems dealt with the fact that I was expecting too much personal attention from my small circle of friends. I would blame my aloneness on them. It is no credit to me, but at some point I made shift from too much dependence on them to looking more after myself. I have been "adopted" as an honorary Grandpa" by a former co-worker and her family. I shared my concerns with her and we then started the process which has led to "meals-on-wheels" and the openness to seek other friendships and perhaps a companion? Well, it could happen.

I have made the conclusion that my tears came

from three sources: grief, depression and anger. The first reaction may be grief. What's the difference, the end result is the same? That wasn't true in my case. When I faced grief, I knew that I did not need to deny the tears, but to focus on what I was grieving for and formulate closure. Grief will follow a pattern and closure will occur.

I then looked at my depression. I love Southern Gospel music; in fact, I played for a quartet years ago from Springfield, Mo. I can immediately lift my spirit by listening to good Southern Gospel music, or, when I had access to a piano, I would play. This was something I could do to challenge the depression. In fairness, I did increase my St. John's Wart. I also made myself talk more openly to my granddaughter and other friends about my loneliness. I have faced my "pity party" sessions and made excellent progress.

My anger was tied to my depression and lack of open communication. I realized that my anger was a product of my youth. I was never been allowed to be angry while growing up. It may be difficult for some readers to understand this, but I was a boy-preacher. I started a public preaching ministry at age 8. All my life I was a "reverend." I was reminded that as a preacher I did not get angry and never said "No" to anyone who asked for help. I was promoted by the church I grew up in. No…you don't need to know the name as I have to axe to grind with them. Nor can I be disrespectfully to my precious Mother who was a praying saint. I was the product of my childhood, just like you are. I realized that in my later life I was spewing the anger I had never been allowed to show when I was young. I understand that this anger could make me a bitter hateful "old" man; or I could embrace it, reduce the effect and make a positive action to allow it to die. This I did by burying a stone as a "scapegoat offering". I now allow myself to feel sad, but not as a lifestyle. I don't blame myself if I over sleep and I do what helps me. One of my great assets is listening to "Talking Books" from the Library of Congress service for the blind. It reminds me of the days when I listened to the radio and used my imagination. This is not done today with the ceaseless noise of television.

My dealing with grief, depression and anger has allowed me to see a new sunrise in my life and not just focus on the sunset. In all this, the vital focus is honesty in dealing with feelings and emotions. When the dust is settled, I discover that my faith is stronger than ever but without the bondage of manmade religion. Perhaps that's another book?

G. Understanding our Limits

Is it a flood or a river? We spend much of our life attempting to improve, enlarge or otherwise promote our skills and abilities to higher and greater limits. The energy and drive for job promotions often rob family life of time with loved ones. Career advancement can often result in broken relationships and family dreams. We are focused to grow, do more, get more and become more than we are. I suppose some of this is acceptable; however, I have seen more damage by this greed and ambition than good. My point is that we are geared to never accept where and what we are. The Apostle Paul put it this way. ***I am not saying this because I am in need, for I have learned to be content whatever the circumstances. I know what it is to be in need, and I know what it is to have plenty. I have learned the secret of being content in any and every situation, whether well fed or hungry, whether living in plenty or in want. I can do everything through him who gives me strength.*** (Phil 4:11-13, NIV)

I know adults that are twisted because their parents never gave them acceptance or approval but demanded and pushed for more perfection or better performance. What a sad gift to leave children. I have seen old business men who don't have the good sense to retire but allow their greed and need to control keep them in the limelight until they are a source of shame and embarrassment to those who know them, both as family and professional associates. We lack the ability to acknowledge limits! I have been forced by blindness to look at and deal with growing limits. This is so contrary to what we are taught by our culture. The sanity of life is to follow the Serenity Prayer: ***God, grant me the serenity to accept the things I cannot change, the courage to change the things I can, and the wisdom to know the difference.*** How true it is and it is a perfect pattern for living.

I have a choice about my limits. My life energy is affected by my choice. My life can follow a positive flow or become a flood of destructive actions. The difference between a damaging flood and a beautiful river is whether the water is following the banks or overflowing with no control. This is true in living. I have watched the reality of not being able to see my pictures on the wall, no longer able to view photos of my parents or to see the faces of my friends clearly. The problem of glare makes going outside an effort of extreme discomfort. Watching television is moving from a visual experience to more of a listening exercise. My use of the computer is slowly diminishing due to glare. I am blessed that I can type by touch and when I can no longer see the computer, I could still write. The hope is that my writing proves to be of value and worth.

The success of accepting limits is related to the ability to continue with what can be done without always regretting the losses. Yes, such losses produce a sense of loss, grief and sadness. I will not be jumping up and down like a kid with a new lollipop, but I also understand that tomorrow will bring new blessings, if I am willing to look ahead and not keep looking back. Looking back not only produces a pain in your neck, but makes you a pain in the neck to your friends. Is it a flood or a river? The choice is yours. Choose wisely.

H. So what if I am cranky? I'm blind!

The tendency to whine, complain and generally bathe in self-pity is much like a weed. It grows without much effort on your part! Self-pity can become a vicious weapon to use against the rest of the world. How easy it is to close your limitation around you as a cape. People can only see the cape and not you! A person with limitations can quickly become a limitation rather than a person with a limitation. I really didn't want to be known as a blind person…but rather a person who is blind. To put it in simple terms; I can either wear my blindness as a focal point for all to see and pity; or I can demonstrate my personhood with blindness as a small part. But, I can immediately hear the cry! Blindness, (my limitation) is not a small part! It's my whole world! How correct!

You can hold a dime so close to your eye that you can't see anything else. But you are holding the dime; now move it back and the rest of the world can be seen! I acknowledge that this is easy to say, but very difficult to do. I often tell my friends that I now have to live and practice what I so lightly preached during my days behind the pulpit. I was a tough preacher!   Don't misunderstand me, the truth remains secure, it is the application that has to be learned. We have a system of guilt theology that is built into much of what we are taught. This is needful when the goal is the control of behavior, and not the understanding of applied grace, forgiveness and the true nature of God (my opinion). When you are guilty you cannot feel worthy or have a healthy self-esteem. No this is not "new Age" where you're OK and I'm OK is the theme. It is the cutting away of the hateful and mean spirited application of theology to ensure the demeaning of the individual. I understand mean-spirited preaching. A loveless message is a condemning message. Self-pity is a vital factor in the removal of self-worth and growing in grace. God forgives, forgets and doesn't hold mistakes against us. He doesn't use the threat or the reminder of them to control our thinking or actions. But we often use this control factor against each other.

So what does all this have to do with self-pity? It makes us the center of all we do or think. I am a poor guilty person and there is nothing I can do except to accept the need to always be wrong! I am blind (limited) and I can do nothing but be enslaved and helpless to this condition. No one can take it away or understand me and my concern…me, me, and me. Let's face it, I'm useless and doomed. So if I am hateful and mean-spirited, you just must accept me as I am. That is me and you can like it or lump it.

I worked in Laredo for four years and used the "handicapped" bus to go back and forth to work. This is the curb to curb service available in most cities as part of the Americans with Disabilities Act. It is a smaller bus adapted for the disabled. It is by appointment and accommodates the passenger's needs. There was a professional medical person in Laredo who was blind and used the bus. I met him once…and that was enough! He was arrogant, rude and mean-spirited. He would not allow anyone to ride the bus with him, but demanded that the driver not accept any other passengers. He expected to be picked up from his office and taken home as the only passenger. Some drivers did honor his hateful demands to avoid his temper and others did not. I was on "his" bus one time. I saw and experienced the personal disgust of being with someone who was consumed by his limitation. I didn't like it and didn't like him. His high education and position lost respect as a result of his banner of blindness and demand for special treatment. My point? He had a choice and so do you.

Yes, I feel sad about my limitations. I feel the frustration of knowing that from week to week I can notice a decline in my vision. I may cry some….I may over sleep some…but I do not have to totally surrender to that sadness. It is easier to slide into the pit of self-pity and then wonder why no one comes around you anymore! I wouldn't visit that person in Laredo for love or money! Wonder why? The effort required to cancel the pity party is a personal decision. I can see a glass half empty or half full. Well, you say that is just playing with words. It doesn't change the reality! Correct, but it changes the ripple effects of that reality. This is not Pollyanna. It is not just saying, I am not blind….it is saying that I will see what I look for. I can look for blessings or curses and I will find them. This is not just a mind game, but an understanding that "nothing happening to me is strange to man".

I did not pay enough attention to the 60 years of good vision and the benefits. I doubt that I expressed thanksgiving over my years of good sight. How sad, but true! We do not miss the water until the well is dry! Now I am learning to value each day and the vision for that day. I could sit in the corner and whine and ask, "Why me?" The questions should be, "Why not me?" This event is a process of life and living. There are millions in the world with the same limitation. My sense of being special cannot be based on the belief that I am beyond problems and pain. I am special because I have the ability to adjust my reaction to my world. I am special because I can use the strength of friends in a positive manner. I am special because my God will supply all my needs.

We have often made the mistake that the purpose of God is to pamper us as a big "sugar daddy (Again, my opinion.)   My Christian teachings allow me to understand that God is my partner in my life-walk allowing me to face each day with His support. This concept came to me years ago. I was Pastor at that time and had to make a visit to a member in the hospital. This person had made a recovery from a serious illness. His had a semi-private room. The curtain was drawn around the other bed. I made the statement to the church member, "You should be so thankful that God has blessed you with a good recovery." That was a perfectly normal "preachy" statement. I then excused myself to leave the room. A man from behind the curtain of the other bed walked behind me. He asked if he could speak to me. I stopped and gave him my attention. "I was sitting by the bed on the other side and heard you. I have a question. A few hours ago my wife died of a disease and I had come to pick up her things. I heard what you said. You were saying that God blessed your church member with recovery. It is your position that I am to accept that has God cursed my wife? Did God like your church member but not me? I have never forgotten my inability to give a cute or clever preachy answer. The belief and acceptance of the Christian faith is not a ticket to "go pass" life and the life process. It is a ticket of companionship and the ability to face each real problem with love and grace.

Yes, I still fight feeling sorry for myself at times. I have learned to apply prayer and quietness to my spirit when these feelings come. The principle: "Be still and know that I am God" has become my anchor. It is not activity than calms the soul, but quiet and open communication to the Father that brings peace. God does not call us to "do"....but to "be". My personal strength comes from knowing my relationship with God....not my activity toward God. If I focus on others, my world has sunshine. If I turn inward, I soon find shadows. The choice is mine. You have the same choice. It is not easy…but is simple.

I will admit that I find myself close to tears often, no not grief or bitterness, but of sheer thanksgiving and gratitude for what I have and can still do. I am not a man of means. I made poor choices and that has impacted my financial world at this stage in my life. I had two divorces and each ex-wife, (one deceased) were good housekeepers. They each kept the house! Funny, sure, but it was reality. I have a good education and should have been pretty well set with finances under normal circumstances. But who or what is normal? It seems now it is the bottom line.

I have a low modest retirement income and a small one-bed room apartment of 700 square feet. This is a huge departure from my 5,000 square foot house of years ago. I own no property, but have no debt except credit cards that are less than the national average and manageable payments. I have no secured debts. I gave up driving over 10 years ago and of course I have no car. The world would say that I am not very successful. I would have agreed years ago…but not now. Greed and material collection is killing the heart and soul of our nation. I know and have worked with individuals who have sold their soul to the devil of greed, riches and accumulation of stuff they never use or have time to enjoy. I have seen greed destroy family relations, turn fathers against sons and daughters. They have empty souls and loveless houses to sit and count their money.

No...I often sit in my small living room and have a sweeping sense of calm, peace and total gratitude for my simple "nest". I will finish my "Meals-on-Wheels" and discover a tear tricking down my cheek in appreciation of this simple meal. (By the way...Meals-on-Wheels deserves your charitable donation. It is truly a great organization.) This is my opinion and experience; and no they didn't know I was going to write this about them. Self-pity? NO...self-appreciation. It could be said that I am becoming a weepy old man? Better than a cranky bitter old goat? It is your choice...nothing forces you.

I. To go to a nursing home or to stay at home. That is the question.

I wore the hat of a Texas Nursing Home Administrator for over 15 years. I served as an Activity Director in Florida. One of the pitfalls of any program that serves the public is the notion that the service or program knows what is best for the consumer! I recall many cases where a person would surrender to the nursing home and the rules and regulations required. It amazes me that a person could have eaten cornbread and milk for supper for 20 years, but as soon as they come under the "protection" of the state, they now must have a balanced meal for supper. The State diet center thinks it knows what's best for ALL residents. They had the right to refuse the meal and the meal is thrown in the trash. Sadly, cornbread and milk could be served. If a person died and left any medication, the all-wise state required that all medication be destroyed. I have seen unopened bottles destroyed. Why…because some third party knew what was best! How many times have I heard the comment from a resident that the "cheery little bubbly activity director was trying to force them to come out of their room to play bingo. I confess I did that more than once myself.

I also noticed the inability of nursing homes and the state to understand the needs of aging eyes. It is required that the floors are always shiny-clean and the overhead lights are fluorescent. This combination makes a glare, the floor looks wet and the light can trigger a seizure. It was often asked why people often fall nursing homes. You tell me. How do you react to a "wet" floor? Oh, also the walls are usually painted white so again welcome to glare city and walk at your old risk. I often fought the battle of lack of color…but was ignored. What's my point? It is easy to fall into the trap of ignoring the wishes of the other person who has limitations and feel that we know what is best for them. The other side of that coin is true. Often people with limits do need encouragement to continue to be involved with activities. So here is the rub. I am content to be at my home. My working career has given me much travel. I worked over 7 years as a Christian Financial Planner and travel on week-ends to a major city to give an all-day seminar each Saturday. I have visited some great places, stayed in fine hotels. In other words I have done the airport, hotel and travel scene. I am very happy to be a home body. I would make some lady a perfect home hubby. I enjoy shopping and unlike most men, I like to walk up and down each row of merchandise. I also enjoy eating out. It doesn't take a rocket expert to figure out that these activities require vision. Take away the vision, or greatly reduce it and you have a formula for staying home.

Let me be more personal, after all this is my book. My eye condition, *retinitis pigmentosa,* (tunnel vision) allows vision straight ahead only. My forward vision is in the normal range corrected by glasses but in the 20/40 range. The problem is the glare effect. I have not found sunglasses effective against glare outdoors. I have to wear two different pair and then only see shadows. I function best under a low level light situation with indirect lights. My apartment is still vision friendly to me. My complaint about going outside stems from the fact that I cannot see. I can see better in the late evening or at night. I walk to check my apartment mail box after 8 P.M. and sometimes at 3 A.M. Moonlight is friendly…could be romantic if I had a partner.

Let me get back to the point. It is amazing to note that the color white seems to be our national color. I cannot see in Walmart to shop…bright lights and white. I made the mistake of going to the bathroom in Walmart and WOW…glare city. I could not found the urinal or the toilet as it all blended into the glare. I had learned that it was necessary to provide contrast for the low vision person. I had replaced my clear drinking glasses with blue and red glasses and replaced white china with dark brown, etc. My apartment also bowed at the national altar of white, so I used a staple gun and hung colored curtain sheers on the walls. I used a green in the living room. I used black around my computer center and green on the others walls…this reduces glare. I have removed a few curtains as my vision continues to dim and I need more light in the room. I also covered my window with the tinting used on cars. These are ways to help low vision people. The problem is that the outside world is not geared for low vision. My friends are great "girl-guides" and until recently my trips out of the house were without much concern. It is a fact that at this point…it is a real effort on my part to go anywhere. I can still see to eat my food on the plate…but everything is blended into glare.

What's my point? I have to balance the desire of friends feeling I need to get out of the house against the lack of enjoyment due to not being able to see anything.. I could get stubborn and simply refuse to go and run the risk of offending my support group. That is not a good option…nor is it a true one. It is a fact that when I do go out with my help, I do enjoy it. I enjoy the interaction with others and feeling that exchange. Isolation is fuel for depression and thoughts of suicide. Again, this is my opinion. I am learning that it is an effort to discover and keep relationships. Duh! We give lip service to that concept but the actual application of that effort appears to be a battle.

We have a large population of older, disabled and sick people who are huddled behind closed doors and finding life to be no more than just waiting to die. I understand this better. I could surrender to that same concept. I had never planned to end myself with no companion or loved one to enjoy watching the sunset with. I had never planned on entering the world of shadows and losing the ability to care for myself. I did not ask for this nor did I welcome it. My blindness is a voice demanding more and more of my attention. I can ignore that voice and sink into the faceless crowd of those who live in despair; or I can adapt, acknowledge and at some point accept the reality of my world. These are choices I can make. It is not easy. I resent not having a companion. I resent having to eat my meals alone, to sleep in bed alone and to wander in my little nest with no one to touch, to feel or to hold. My blindness has not reduced my human need for human interaction. I have even joined some dating sites on the internet. You got to be kidding? I'll talk about that in more detail later.

The person with limitation must make some effort. This is a simple fact…but it is hard to know how to reach out. I am sorry to say, that the answer is so simple and yet so complicated. The simple answer is communication. Talk to those who are in your world. I have spent my life using words. I preached, I sold, I counseled others, I taught others at the public, private and college level…and yet I had to learn how to ask for help. This led me to Meals on Wheels as I had to face the fact that I could no longer see to cook safely. I admitted to my Granddaughter my great fear. She was with me as I opened up to ask for this help and also to admit I needed to reach out to others. I am now waiting for additional opportunities to be explained to me to reach out to others. The bottom line is this: sometimes other people do know what is good for you, maybe even what is best, but in the final chapter you have to make the decision to act or die. Banging your head against the cabinet door is not the answer.

The trip into the world of darkness is a lesson in self-examination of feelings and emotions. I awake each morning, or near noon, with the growing awareness that I can see less than the day before or the week before. I know the annoyance of walking into my open pantry door or of hitting my head on an open cupboard door. This hasn't happened often. When it has it has been a flash of anger, resentment and a little pain. Once I walked into the door frame of the bathroom. Man…what a jerk! It is bad enough to have to rush to the bathroom and then to bounce off the door jam. Give me a break? I once walked into my large closet thinking it was the bathroom. It didn't take long to notice the difference in the fixtures in the room. Yes, I made it to the bathroom without accident.

What is my point?   This is a real trip taken by a real person with real fears. Yes, I understand the Bible teachings and I have preached the life of trust and to lean on the Good Lord. This is true. This is correct. This is much harder to practice than to preach. Today started badly. I have discovered that it takes a long time for my eyes to focus and it seems to be talking longer each day. When my "Meals on Wheels" arrived I was unable to tell what was on the plate. I could see shapes but could not tell what it was. OK, so my meals can now be a surprise! We ALL like surprises!

Watching television is less and less of an

enjoyment as I am just watching shadows move on screen. How easy it is to panic and allow my mind to go wild. What happens when I am totally in the dark? What I feel is a mixture of fear, panic, resentment and loss of hope or desire to face the future. Does that sound like a good Christian? My past teachings do not serve me well. A good Christian is always happy, chipper, up-beat and clapping hands of praise and worship. Move over Job; make room on your sack cloth and ashes. My real feelings demand to be addressed. I am a firm believer that we behave according to what we believe. The guilt-ridden theology often pushed down our throat does not allow for honest exploration of feelings. We can use Bible verses to accuse, to shame or to otherwise negate the expression of honest feelings. It is true, "the truth shall set you free", however; you have to face the truth and not an imposter. I don't want to be blind. I don't want it to get worse and worse. I don't want to wonder how and where I am going to live. I don't want to lose my ability to enjoy the sights of life. I am interested in discovering my resentment. I find that I can resent my friends who are "normal" who don't have to deal with the pain I do. Sounds like the beginning of a pity party? All the negative gloom and doom that can be piled in a heap becomes available for spreading over my world. What am I saying? I didn't ask for this nor did I make any provisions for it. I can understand the prayer of Jesus, "Father, if it be possible, take this cup from me". I have prayed that prayer. I have also prayed "why have you forsaken me?" The marvel is that these are expressions of honesty which can be touched by the reality of the truth of Scripture. It is the phony cheerleader style of believing that destroys the power of Grace.

I have to review the principle, "sufficient unto the day, is the evil thereof". The fact is today has the portion of problems and concerns assigned to it. We destroy hope and growth when we try to add tomorrow's fears and yesterday's guilt to the daily load. It becomes too much. I must live one day at a time. I will tell you that even while I write this…I am not the picture of a happy camper jumping up and down with joy! I am aware that what I am writing is true and at some point that truth will seal my fears. Time is better spent making adjustments in lifestyle rather than trying to hang on to the past. This will mean, in my case, to review my food pantry and start giving away those items I can no longer cook safely. The act of giving is a healing act. I can bless my friends with my acknowledgement and active involvement with my limitations. Do you need a pressure cooker?

The world does not promote honest expressions in general. We are taught to be worried about what people will think of us. We are geared to always be aware of how other people may see us. We learn that we must be concerned that people will like us. I could go on and on. The problem with all this is simple. We do not learn to have self-esteem unless it is given to us by others. We are encouraged to find our personal worth by external methods. Eve in the Garden was told that she was not complete and needed the "apple" to "make her like God". This was the first marketing program to mankind. She questioned that she was complete just by having a relationship with God. She needed ownership of the "apple". This lie has been the downfall of mankind. We are all ownership driven. You have heard often that you will feel better, look better and be better by buying this or that. We are never told that we are acceptable just as we are. We need to color our hair, lose weight, gain weight, get a boob job, get a new hat, a new dress, a new car or a bigger house. We strive to fulfill this race to success only to discover at the end we are just exhausted and empty. I have been by the bedside of many dying people. I have never heard a dying person request that the gold watch be put in his hand, the copy of the latest contract won or the keys to the car be given. I have heard, "I wish we had taken that vacation, spent more time with the children, used the fine china more, and burned the pretty candle". You get my drift. It is the lack of relationships that starves the soul. I have known many wealthy individual. I have worked for a few. I have watched them suffer the soul death of selling out to greed and self-centered living. The wealth gave no peace but mocked them that they needed more.

You don't have to go blind to understand the value of your relationship. Renew your love to your wife, children and family. Put the work world back in proper order to that it supports your relationships and doesn't replace them. Walk with your loved one and smell the roses or the onions, whatever. Hold hands and fill your soul with the joy of belonging. Allow your faith to affect your lifestyle. It is sad that our modern world is trying to destroy anything of past value. The effort to destroy God in our Nation is sad and stupid. The attempt to rewrite history to wipe out certain unhappy facts is an attempt to ignore truth and honesty. The political system in America has become corrupt and greedy to the extent that the middle class and poor are simply a hindrance to be removed as soon as possible.

My walk into the world of darkness has made me keenly aware of the value and soul enriching quality of relationships. I have been blessed with a small circle of people who care and relate to me. This small circle is responsible for my continued well-being. I thank God daily for them. The truth of the matter is that relationships become more valuable as my vision dims. The "things" can no longer feed my ego since I can't see them. The ownership of things quickly loses appeal. I can no longer see any details of my apartment in terms of my living room furniture, decorations on the wall or pictures. I used to have a "Wall of Fame" that I hung over 90 frames showing college degrees, awards, newspaper clippings, telegrams from governors/senators and organization memberships as symbols of my "success". I am a little embarrassed as I think about how I must have "paraded" these in front of anyone who came to my home. Slowly they became more of a burden as I moved from place to place and slowly they vanished. I have less than a dozen and I can't see them now. I will probably throw them also. Oh   wait….I can hear someone say…they are important. They are a part of who you were. Never let rid of stuff. Oh, give me a break! They are a part of the past. We learn from the past, but must move on. Living in the past can become a prison and a poison. Yes, they were a part of who I was. They are not who I am. I have no one to impress anymore. We don't need to impress each other but should learn to embrace each other. If you come to see me, my walls may be clean and empty?

SENSELESS, but NOT STUPID!

The world reveals itself to us by our 5 senses. We taste, we see, we touch, smell and we hear. The combination of senses makes the world personal to us. I doubt that many of us give much attention to these senses while they are functioning well. The breakdown of any sense calls attention to the value. A good friend made the casual comment that I was "losing senses". I had never thought of my situation in that framework. The truth is that two of my senses were in revolt: my eyesight and my hearing. It is common for a person having vision problems to also have hearing issues as well. I had worn hearing aids for years. So I am functioning on 3/5 of my senses. The image of a car motor with knocking pistons came to my mine. The car motor can be repaired….I cannot! The common understanding is that when a sense gives up, the others tend to "buck up" and try to compensate. I haven't been in my valley long enough to notice any "troops" coming to the rescue. I do have a keen awareness of how much I miss the vision. The hearing hasn't really upset me that much. I figure I don't mind what I don't hear! My hearings aids make the difference and I wear them only when I feel I don't want to miss anything. I have to confess that the lack of vision does lead to a sense of "confusion" and perhaps downright stupid behavior. My ability to walk is affected by this vision lack. I could be described as a "drunk" walking but without the benefit of the booze. When I first wake up, it takes my eyes a long time to focus; I have discovered myself walking into the closet rather than the bathroom. This does not make the "smart meter" go very high.

My greatest awareness of my limitation is when I go outside. I have described my problem with glare. The best way to describe it, in my opinion, is to equate it to "snow-blindness". I immediately see nothing but a bright light. It is not the bright light seen by those who have a "near-death" experience as they approach "Heaven". My case is not so lofty. To give an example of the close tie to vision and walking let me give you this true example. This happened last week, well, not this last week, but the last week at the time of this writing. My apartment complex has a very nice "mail-shelter" containing all the mail boxes of the complex. The shelter is about 120 steps from my front door. (Blind people do learn to count!) I generally wait until after 7 or 8 p.m. to make the trip. I can see in the dusk and also with moonlight. I decided to check my mail earlier. I may have been 4. I put on 3 pair of sunglasses and as I looked out my door, I was able to see shapes and the sidewall. I walked toward the shelter and the crosswalk painted white leading to the mail boxes. I was forcing myself to keep focused on the ground to locate the white cross walk. The clouds must have parted for suddenly I became totally immersed in brightness. I lost my sense of direction and the annoying panic became a partner. The bottom line is I was lost. In the past when I have walked to the mail box I could count on 2 or 3 cars driving by. I could go at 3 a.m. and somebody would drive by. Do you think anybody was out and about now? Of course not! It took me about 20 minutes to find my apartment door less than 100 footsteps away. I was totally wiped out. I have done this once before and was caught by a neighbor as I was headed for the street. Who would have thought that walking in a straight line or a correct line can be affected by your vision? I waited until 11 P.M. to go back. The feeling of control is important to most of us. I have discovered that I can feel the urge to throw a "fit" when I wake up and can't see in my room. Frustration, anger and general disgust can overwhelm me. I know better than to whine or feel pity. Knowing and doing is not always the same thing.

We depend on our senses for planning our life. I am senseless and trying to learn positive adjustments without despair. I do well some days....I fail on other days. What can I say? I have learned another lesson that is vital, in my opinion. We have 5 senses given to us by our Creator. I have discovered that a sixth sense has been developed for many of us. The sense of guilt! I have commented on this but it is worth additional review. I was reared in a loving home with a mother and father who loved me. I was informed from the time I was old enough to understand that I was adopted. My mother used to tell me that they "chose" me and did not "have" to have me. I had the normal desire to know about my adoption as I got older but mom would not discuss it. I somehow learned that she was afraid that I might not love her as much if I knew about my adoption. I didn't force the issue.

Allow me to time travel ahead to about age 40 to the time of my Dad's death. My mother's sister, my aunt, had been close to my family. My mom was the oldest of 14 children and was a second mom to most. She and this sister were close and we often visited. I would spend my summers playing with her 2 daughters and one son. She was close. I asked her about my adoption and she offered me the following story. My mother was unable to have children due to health issues. Remember this is 1941 and medical cures were limited. Mom prayed for years to have a son and promised God she would give the child back to Him. It appears that her cousin impregnated his girlfriend. She was only 15 and he was 17. Her father became angry and would not allow the couple to marry as they wished to. The child-mother was placed under house arrest and the boy was not allowed to visit. The baby was born and immediately the "grandfather" took the child in one hand and a rifle in the other, and delivered the child to the boy-father. The girl-mother grieved herself to death and the boy kept the baby for a few days with no clue how to care for an infant. He remembered that his cousin, who had married a baker, had been praying for a child. When the child was 8 days old, he took the infant to his cousin with the promise that if she would take him, he would never interfere. This was the story given to me as my history.

True to her word Mom dedicated me to the Lord and she devoted her life to her "God-gift". I was her answer to prayer and the church became my second home. I always knew that I would be a preacher and started preaching at our local church at age 8. Was this a true call or the fulfillment of a praying mother? Looking back…it doesn't matter. The events and actions were real and sincere to me. My parents gave me much love but I was carefully taught to act, look, think and behave as a preacher. I wore a suit to school and all during school was known as "Preacher Boy". I had a tent for revivals during my Junior High and High School days. There were many young people promoted by the church during that time. I started wearing glasses at 8 or perhaps younger. My eye disease may have been present at that time. I was well promoted and preaching became my focus in life. I devoted my life to the preaching ministry for over 20 years. I became what I was taught and learned to be a "hard line" preacher. I have not mentioned the name of the church as I have no reason to throw any rocks. I made the decisions I made so I have no need to blame any church or group. I grew up in a strict legal atmosphere. I was not allowed to dance, go to movies, play games, believed God would strike you dead if you touched a can of beer and you had to always remember you were a sinner. The guilt theology is strong in many groups and becomes a sixth sense for many. How sad.

My sense of guilt was gospel-based and the

underlining basis for preaching. I was successful as a "defender of the faith" when actually I was mean-spirited and hateful. One of my sad memories that lives with me today is how mean I was to a couple I married in Hartford, CT. I am going to give actual details. You will understand why at the end of the story. I was Pastor of The Hartford Gospel Tabernacle in Hartford, CT. A young couple came to ask me to marry them. She was pregnant. I told them that they could not use the main sanctuary, but I would permit them to use the small side chapel. (Remember, I was the sheriff of the kingdom and sex outside of marriage was a sin). My board applauded my defense of the faith. I married the couple and during the ceremony I made the following statement, I still remember it today. "While we cannot condone the circumstances that bring this couple together, we do honor the love present". Slap, slap, slap. The bride's face was stunned and the mother of both reacted. I believe this happened during the late 60's or early 70's. I honestly cannot remember the dates I was there. I would love to locate that couple and apologize for being such a jackass, as Matlock liked to say. I was so wrong and it still brings tears to me as I understand how hateful that was. God has forgiven me…but I would welcome the opportunity to ask the couple to forgive.

This development of guilt is a solid foundation in many people. The guilt-theology churches use guilt to make people give money, attend church and do "churchy" things. We do not allow people to drop their past and move to their future. The Bible clearly teaches that God forgives and forgets. We only have to ask forgiveness once. "As far as the east is from the west" is the promise of killing our past. God never uses it against us. Who is the accuser of the brethren? It is Satan. The fact is that as soon as you ask God to forgive you it is done. God no longer remembers it about you and certainly doesn't hold it against you. That is not the way we deal with each other. We never let people walk away from their past. The church has continued to make second rate Christians of those who are divorced or have had past addictive problems. We refer to their past, they are not allowed to teach Sunday school, be ordained or to walk in any sense of freedom. This is wrong. I did it and I was wrong. If anyone can find that young couple I abused, please contact me at: fredcullens@yahool.com.

The escape from guilt requires great effort. It requires a change in our thinking habits and often leaving people who are not good for us and seeking others to help embrace freedom. The ability to adjust to life's "lemons" in a positive manner may often depend on the ability to give up past guilt. God is not the mean-spirited hateful and revengeful deity we are often taught. Nor is He a sugar daddy to be a foundation of Pollyanna roses and tulips. The correct understanding of His love and concern can make our human experience full and honest. Fear is replaced with a love embrace. I can get angry at God because of my blindness and never get beyond the death knell of sorrow. He will allow me to make that choice.

I have learned to be thankful for my parents, my past, even the bad, and to understand that each day is my opportunity to see flowers or weeds. One more interesting note about my childhood and loving parents is that I never knew much about my Father's side of the family. They were in Mississippi and we lived in Oklahoma. Early this year my friends had me make a comment on Facebook. I received a message asking if I was the son of Fred F. and Lovis Cullens. It turned out that this was from a cousin that I had not seen since 1967. I almost remembered him. We had a good time catching up on family matters from my Father's side. I told my cousin the story about my birth. He was quiet. He then told me that the story was not exactly what the family had been told by my father. He asked if I wanted to hear and of course I did.

My cousin told me that my Dad told his mother and she told my cousin and the rest of the family. Dad did marry a wonderful lady who could not have children. She was very close to her next sister who spent much time with them. It was agreed that this sister would bear a child for them. She and Dad formed me. I was then adopted and the rest was history. The first story of my birth had been told to me by this aunt…who was my birth mother. It did make sense. Is had wondered why my aunt was so close to Mom and Dad. The thought even closed my mind that perhaps my aunt and Dad had an affair? Why I thought that? I have not a clue…but then I understood all the time spent with my cousins who were actually my half-brother and half-sisters. I have no reason not to accept this version since it came from the family. I do marvel at the love underscoring this whole affair.   This was 1941 with much different moral standards. I have to marvel at the relationship between my adopted mother and the birth mother, her sister. My conclusion is that I have been blessed with much love in my life and I am thankful. I need to continue to destroy the sixth sense of guilt. God is in control. I may not always be happy about the circumstances and that is allowed by His Love. You don't have to be blind to start the process of destroying any guilt. Go for it.

LOVE IS BLIND! WELL, SO AM I! WHAT'S YOUR POINT?

The world loves a lover! That's what some poet said a long time ago. The subject of love has been the focus of hundreds and hundreds of books and poems. The human experience is touched by love from the time of birth. The acceptance or suspicious approach to love can affect our quality of life and living. I believe in love and love the possibility of being in love and loving. We embrace many levels of love. We love from a family position, love mother, father, brother and sister. We love those who share our goals and interests. We can develop plutonic love relationships all during our life. These help to balance the process of enduring life and living.

We also have some pretty dumb ideas about love. The one area which has been greatly abused is the sexual love. The moment I say sex, many of you are now uncomfortable. I grew up during the time when sex was not discussed, explained or made a topic of conversation unless it was associated with guilt and "no no". I don't embrace the "free love" of the hippy group but I am ashamed of the "shame" teachings that prevailed during my younger years. My experience has been that the church has done a very poor job of teaching about sex and about money. In the first, just don't, and in the second just give to the church. We taught our kids to be ashamed of their body parts and gave them foolish names. The boys had "woo-woo's", or "johnson's" and the girls had "tee-tee" o or "twat" for their "private parts". The usage of penis or vagina was filled with horror and shame. How stupid! This history of shame teaching led to poor marriages and couples unable to find any freedom or growth in their sexual love life.

I just explain that I do not make the assumption that love and sex are the same. Plutonic love has no sexual interaction and sex may be performed without love. I was taught that sexual intercourse outside of marriage is wrong, and I have lived my life according to that concept.

I like women and made no apology for that! I am amazed that some people feel that just because I am 70 years old, I have become sexless. Having said that, I must confess that I have never been very courageous in my sex life. I am saddened to look back and realize that I have been alone for over 22 years. I mean alone! I have to go back over 10 years to even discover any "dating petting". Now that is sad! This may be too much information? I now find myself living a life of the solitary and true regret. Let's understand the difference between sexual and sensual. A simple distinction could be that being sexual captures the eye and sensually captures the soul and spirit.

The general pathway for us to be sexually attracted to someone is to see them. The shape of the body, the color of the hair, the eyes, the smile and the tempting movements of the body ignite passion. But wait, those signals are no longer available for the blind or the severely vision impaired. I have always been attracted to the open faced, bright smile and eyes of a woman. I guess I notice the face first and the eyes and smile. The rest follows in due course. Now what do I do? I am at the point that I can dimly see a person's face encased in a hazy glare reminiscent of Saints. I see the same dim face when looking in the mirror to shave. The face is hazy. So what is the attraction now? I have already discussed that I have to approach people without my preconceived thoughts; this is also true in terms of seeking a sexual partner. To be honest I don't have any direct answers, as I haven't sought anyone yet. I have not been in a position to meet anyone. My social world has been greatly reduced to my circle of support friends who I depend on for survival and not for companionship or sexual fulfillment.

I can only describe what I don't like at this point. I don't like not having the touch of a woman. Yes, my friends give me a hug and I appreciate that, but I miss the step beyond. I hate coming to the end of each day alone. I hate sleeping alone as I have for over 22 years. I miss the side of my nature that yearns to hold, to kiss and to show affection. I have always been a very emotional person. I have no problem expressing my feelings. I have the little "nagging" of someone who notices whether my socks match or my pants match my coat. I miss the calm that comes by having someone to enjoy a movie, a music tape or a sunset. The bottom line is that being alone is not my wish; however, I must confess and admit it has been my choice. I am learning that we are responsible for our circumstances. I had no choice over the fact of my eye disease; however, I must assume ownership of how I "ride" the ebb and flow of my vision. I look back and wish I had gone out and been more assertive about dating instead of making my work too time consuming. Sound familiar?

So what do I do now? Frankly, I don't know. I know that I am no longer "hooked" on looks. I now perceive people less from their physical side but more from the character and "vibes" I can sense. Does that sound a wee bit woo, woo? A little spooky? I don't think so and if it is, it is my reality. I have very little to offer a companion in terms of material goods. I can't even offer much in terms of helping, as I need help myself. So, do I dare hope for a relationship again for the sexual-sensual side of life? My honest answer is, I don't know. But it is a real need of the human spirit. I could deny it, become bitter and withdrawn and never explore that need. That is a formula for successful depression and a loss of any spark of life. I guess I need to discover that someone who is blind to my limitations and can allow me to love. So maybe it is a good thing, Love is blind?. I have no answers but I dare not deny the reality of that human need. Who knows? It has been said that people are looking for love in all the wrong places, maybe since I can't see where I am looking...love will find me? One can hope.

WHO'S AFRAID OF THE DARK?
I AM, SOMETIMES.

It may not be very manly to admit that I become fearful and downright afraid, but I do! I understand the teachings that we are to "fear not" "perfect love removes fear" and the other true teachings from Sunday school. These are true, but often it takes time to allow the application to become a light in the dark. I never had a clue that my sunset in life would be in the dark. We do not know what the future holds and that is good. My trip down the shadow path started about 10 years ago and I do not know if it will end in total blackness or not. It doesn't matter as the future will be what it will be.

What am I afraid of? I have faced new and unplanned fears over the past few months. I wake up each morning not knowing how effective my vision will be. I am aware that my sight is less than 1 month ago. I am now barely able to see across a room in my apartment. I have discussed my awareness that it is no longer safe for me to cook hot food. I can't see water boiling or the control knob on the stove. Meals on Wheels have become my main meal. I am afraid of not being able to shave. I am afraid of not being able to live alone anymore. I am afraid that I will have to be a burden on someone for my care. I don't want to think about not being able to see my plate of food anymore. I am afraid of how to take a shower if I can't see anything.

Am I afraid of the dark? Yes, I am and no I'm not. When I feel my fear I can also feel my anger. I did not ask for this "cross" to bear nor do I want to be enslaved by it. I am afraid that I will not be able to meet another lady to love me. I am an object of need rather than a source of help.   I am afraid that my identity and self-wroth will be lost in the night. Yes, I get afraid.

I can do one of two things with this fear. I can curl up and hope and pray to die quickly, which I have done, or I can reveal the fear and embrace it so I can defuse the power of fear. The problem of denial is that I can soon become angry and resentful of my friends. They have companions; they have the joy of living. I can misdirect my anger toward them and speed up the destruction of my world.

I have learned if I talk about my fear to someone and the fear loses some power. I also have learned that you don't ALWAYS talk about your fear or people will soon avoid you. Sharing is not putting down roots. There are things I can do to reduce the power of fear. If I listen to Southern Gospel Music I am swept into a wave of peace and joy. I can listen to my "talking books" and time zooms by. I can spend time writing this "book" and time will whiz by. I think I am learning that activity will challenge fear. I can review my understanding of Biblical truth and allow the words to grow without guilt in my mind.

I am afraid that someday I will wake up in the dark

and there will be no hand to hold on to. I can allow that fear to grow and destroy my world, or I can understand that God will always provide what I need, when I need it and not a second before. This is a leap of faith. If I leap in the dark, I permit myself to be caught. If I tremble on the edge of darkness, I assure my failure.

Who's afraid of the dark? I am, but I will allow you to share by being open and honest. The bottom line is still true; our faith is given to us to be used, to be leaned on and not to simply set on a shelf. My faith is my anchor, even when I am afraid.

THANK GOD AND DUCT TAPE!

I need to remind you that I am not totally "bat" blind but severely restricted. The correct term for my condition, I guess, would be severely visually challenged. I do meet definition of "blindess" according to the Social Security Disability guidelines. That was the basis to start receiving my Social Security Disability Benefits when I was 62. The person who is experiencing the lack of vision is aware of that limitation at all times. It is amazing how much energy is spent trying to see.

The lack of vision does allow you to become creative, if you want to. I have described a few of my efforts to assist my vision, but let me explore that option a little deeper. My particular eye condition requires low level lighting. I can see straight ahead but have no ability to accommodate any glare. My forward vision is additional hampered by a fuzzy perception. This is the effect of my "tunnel" closing in. I am told that the percentage of those with RP that go totally blind is very low. I do hope so!

I have made concession to keep my ability to live alone alive and well. I have 6 lamps in my 13 x 13 living room. I have switched the bulbs from 100 watt to 60, to 40 and soon will go to 30. My condition is best served by more lights at a dimmer level. Indirect lighting is the ideal! I have two large windows in my little apartment nest. I have covered the windows with the tinting that you use on car windows and also covered my television. I hate high definition! So much for progress!

The desired goal for the vision-impaired is contrast. I hate the color white but it appears that the whole world loves it. Take note and see how white the world is! I use colored place mats on my little dining arm. I replaced my white dishes for colored. I can't see a clear glass of water. I switched my glassware to ruby red and cobalt blue.

The problem of the bathroom is adjusted by using colored towels on the rods and over the tub. I have a colorful toilet set that covered the white toilet and that makes it safe. My light over the sink was the décor light with three screw-in bulbs that shined directly in my face. The apartment maintenance man built a "box" over the lights. The light is now forced upward and I can now see my dull face. I am still able to use my computer by adjusting all fonts and images to larger sizes.

The ability to adjust and adapt to changing conditions is an act of the will. I have always been blessed with a good mind. I usually don't have to be told anything more than two times. I had an employer who stated that my mind was like a "steel trap". I can't stand repetition. I think that goes back to my childhood and my dear mother's tendency to "wear out" telling me when I had done wrong. Let me give an example.

One time I tried to get a cookie out of the cookie

jar and I knocked it to the floor and it broke into many pieces. Mom had told me not to get a cookie before supper. She asked me why I disobeyed and asked again, "didn't I tell you not to get a cookie?" Six months later, "why did you get that cookie?" Do you get my drift? That long enduring verbal punishment made me very resentful of anything being repeated. I can understand the first time. I have little tolerance for those people who have to tell you the same thing 5 different ways. I got it the first time, now, move on. My memory and my strong organizational habits serve me well. I can find stuff in the dark by knowing where I put them. This is why I must organize my own kitchen, pantry and refrigerator. I have learned to pour my coffee or milk without overflowing the cup or glass. This is done by simply putting my finger inside so I can feel the liquid. OK, I won't stick my finger in your glass!

I am grateful for the blessing of the big black permanent marking pen. I am able to adjust my air conditioning as I can see the BIG "C" for cool and "H" for heat. The apartment did replace my control box with a large print one.   I have been blessed by finding an apartment complex that truly cares about the residents. If you ever want to live in Midland, Texas, consider Silver Creek Apartments. The present management is a delight to deal with. They have been nice to me.

Anyway, back to the issue. I have learned to count while outside.   The outdoor glare makes it almost impossible for me to see outside. I wear two or three pair of sunglasses and still cannot go during the day. The evening or late at night are the best time for me to vampire out. I know that it is 20 steps beyond the dumpsters to make a left turn to walk to the office to deposit mail. It is 10 steps from the last carport post to the sidewalk leading to the mail shack. It is 100 steps from the mail shack to my apartment door…or a left turn after the speed bump. Confused? These little tricks are known to most vision-impaired people.

I discovered that my refrigerator had died during a Friday night. I did not make the discovered until mid-morning on Saturday when I poured a glass of milk. It was warm. Yuk! My freezer, which was not full, had soggy packages and the contents of the fridge were warm. I don't need to describe the smell of the mayo and other items that love the cold and die in the heat. I called the office and it was determined that the compressor was dead. Well, duh! I threw away the spoiled food and was told that it would be Monday before a replacement could be installed. That's cool! Monday came and I had a brand new Frigidaire. Neat, but I had the same problem with glare when I opened the door. I could not see anything but white glare. Darn the color white. Look in your fridge! What to do?

As anyone knows the only two items needed to survive are duct tape and WD-40 lubricant and penetrating oil. If it is stuck then you can use WD-40. If it wiggles duct tape it. A few weeks earlier I had purchased some black duct tape to have the Meals on Wheels sign stuck to my window for the driver to find me. I could not put the sign on the inside as the apartment complex has back privacy screens on the windows. You can see out but no one can see it. The duct tape worked perfectly. My little brain made a determination and I torn off a length of duct tape and covered the edges of the shelves in the fridge. I also covered the edge of the two storage bins at the bottom. Walla…thanks God and duct tape. I can now see where to put stuff. Thank God for my creative mind and the duct tape for its' sticky side.

IF SLEEPING HEALS THE BODY, I SHOULD LIVE FOREVER!

How do you pass time? It is interesting how we measure time. It is a common experience that when you are very busy that time seems to rush by. The typical 'rat race" of our lifestyle does not include training or tolerance for "free time". It is true that millions of dollars are spent promoting vacation, leisure time and relaxation; however, few learn the technique of actually enjoying time. Have you noticed that when you meet someone for the first time that you soon ask the question, "What do you do?" We have a need to know where that person is located on the "pecking order" in terms of where we are. We tend to decide how we will relate to people based on this knowledge of "what do you do?" No, this isn't an indictment, but rather a statement of fact!

We have been conditioned to believe that the value and worth of an individual is measured by what they do. The brain surgeon is certainly more important that the person who drives the trash truck? The highly placed politician is to be listened to more carefully than the greeter at Walmart? This focus on what we do becomes a problem as we grow older and the "doing" gets more difficult due to the normal aging process. I have witnessed the sadness of working with or knowing men who did not realize when their time of "doing" was over. They continued to "do" and sadly ruined what good they had "done". I have watched this sad fact in those who have sold their soul to the god of greed, control and self-centeredness. How sad! They never had respect to begin with but now they reap pity, ridicule and embarrassment by those to know or have to work with them.   The problem with living only for what we do is that this does not produce or promote solid self-esteem. It produces a nagging fear of having to hang on, out-do or otherwise reduce the value or contribution of others who might out shine our "doing". This can fracture families, destroy friendships and maintain an attitude of anger, resentment and distrust.

When I find myself unable to "do"…what then is

my value and purpose in living? This question confronts the retiree as a normal part of readjusting from a "work" world to "home" world. The old fear is that if a person stops working they will die soon afterward. There is no question that examples can be presented to underscore this concept; however, it may also be discovered that other it is the fault of the person for not enlarging his/her world. I have watched "great" men in businesses who are babies, when it comes to any involvement outside the work world. This is sad and often these people are in positions of control over others who must endure their shortsightedness. You know who I mean, you have worked for them! My value as a person cannot be built on what I do. This is a formula for defeat when the time comes when I can no longer "do" what I did.

If you will go with me to the story in Genesis about Adam and Eve, you may discover that it was God's perfect will that these people enjoy an open relationship with Him. They were caretakers but not owners. It has to be noted that they had to live on fruits, nuts, etc…as nothing was killed until they violated the rules and discovered they were naked. I wonder if this is an insight into the fact that eating less meat is better for us.

Adam and Eve were perfect and living in a perfect world and void of any hint of wrong, guilt or shame. This changed after they accepted the lie that they "needed" more than what they had. Eve was told that they were be like God, new and improved? This was the first marketing plan presented to the human race. We are never told that we are good enough, tall enough or clever enough. We must buy a certain car, wear certain clothes, and accumulate "things" in order to improve our life and world. What a crock! I have seen the scars on the life of the young man who never had the approval of his Dad who never felt the son was enough! The sadness in the young lady who was denied any acceptance, encouragement or nurturing from a cold, competitive and selfish parent. They could never "do" enough to measure up.

The choice of how we use time is always present. My slow loss of vision has made me more aware of how important it is to understand the proper use of time. The American rat-race promotes total abandonment to the world of work. This miss-shapes the soul! I have slowly realized that my ability to "do" is affected by my ability to see. I used to love to read. I can't see well enough to enjoy reading anymore. I loved to collect, but I can no longer see the collections. I love to cook. It is now a dangerous function for me to deal with fire, boiling water or a hot oven. I loved to window shop, yes, I am a man, but now I can't see the windows anymore. I enjoy eating out…but it is more and more stressful as I can't see well enough to be a gracious diner. Soon it will be more stressful and embarrassing than enjoyable.

What is the value and purpose of my life now?

My identity has been labeled in the past by my function as a minister, a teacher, a stockbroker, a financial planner, a hospital/nursing home administrator, a Social Security Disability Specialist, Reverend Cullens and simply Dr. Fred. This gave structure to my world and meaning to my living. Now what do I do and who am I?

My early reaction was to be angry and plunge into depression. Tears and internal rage were constantly brewing inside. Panic, fear and resentment became my daily companions. These were magnified by the limited circle of friends I had remaining. My world was over and I truly wanted to die. Yes, I considered suicide, but I am not into pain, so only thought about it. I went days without seeing or talking to anyone. I discovered that excessive sleeping would make time go by. I have slept the entire week-end away. I slept so much that I became physically weak from not eating and had to franticly find something to eat before my blood sugar bottomed out. This was a dark and terrible time! I was forced to seek help and was blessed by just enough friends that cared about me to keep poking themselves into my world.

I hope I have given you a picture of the despair of the results of living to "do" without understanding that balance is the goal in life. I like the example that the chicken that produced the eggs for breakfast was involved, but the pig that provided the ham was committed. We need to be involved in the work world, but not committed. Yes, I know, this flies in the face of what we are taught. Look at the end results. I have worked for the goal in life. I have worked for 4 employers who were wealthy, powerful and successful. They were also greedy, controlling and mean-spirited toward everyone, even their families. They were sad and lonely yet were pitifully rich, but poor. They only lived for work. They had no sense of "who" they were in terms of relationship. They knew only "what" they were in terms of ownership and unfulfilled greed and wanton accumulation of things. They were as the rich man who built bigger barns to hold his "things", only to die.

What is my point? I am looking back at the progress of my blindness and slowly learning that the loss of certain abilities happens to everyone. When I review the reality of life, it becomes clear that life has "seasons". We are taught that in the Bible. The oak leaf doesn't scream as it falls from the tree. The faded rose continues to smell until gone. They have no choice, you say. That is true. They are responding to how they were made. We have the option to choose how we respond. Like it or not, our world is shaped by our free-will choices and not by a stern unbendable God in the sky!

It is true that I did not vote to be blind, no more than I can vote for it to rain or snow tomorrow. I did not vote to be 5'8" or to have blue eyes, but I never "threw a fit" about that. So why do so now? God did not promise nor does the Bible teach that life is easy or fair. Those who dwell on the "prosperity" gospel are only lining their own pockets. We are promised a relationship with God. The promise is that He will "never leave nor forsake us". The path of life can be rough or smooth but we have a relationship as "sons and daughters". This is to be our identity. Who we are and whose we are. These are the foundation stones of a successful life. Paul taught that he had learned to be content whether he had a lot or a little it was godliness with contentment. We don't honor contentment in our rat race world. We push for more, so we need a bigger house; we strive for more so we need to work longer hours to pay for the excess. I am learning the freedom of enjoying what I have rather than the panic of what I don't have.

If you have a wife, you should love her and understanding your blessing. I know the lack and loss of a loved one. If you have your family, you should spend time and energy with them. Be free with your support, love and praise. Forget the perfection! I have been by the bedside of many as they died. I have heard the remorse of not spending time with the family, of not taking vacations and of making work too important.

I do not like being alone. I know the rational comments, but the bottom line is that we were created for fellowship and not solitude. Bitterness and resentment has colored many people due to their experiences. I could be bitter over my past failed relationships. I could mourn and deep dive into the muddy water of self-pity and poor-me; but this does not affect the reality of my world. I made choices and I can choose how to respond to my world. It is said, if life gives you lemons, then make lemonade. I say, if you don't like lemonade, then sell it.

I have not become bitter or hateful about love and relationship as many have. I could! But it only affects me and not the others. So at some point it is time to grow up, look up and walk in the light and not in darkness. A choice! I am learning the art of thanksgiving. I have more days that I wake up with a prayer of thanks on my lips. I am overwhelmed with gratitude when my hot meal arrives from "Meals on Wheels". I am thankful for strangers who are cooking my food, delivering the same and without expecting anything from me. I am learning to listen to my inner self and my body. We need to learn the healing power of quiet listening. We can touch "the Christ in you" if we shut up, sit down and just listen! Not the American way? I will wake up knowing what I want to eat for breakfast based on what my body is demanding.

I still have some problems with too much time and not enough activity to fill it. I watch television and some DVD movies. They are becoming more and more mere shadows but I can still enjoy them. I can still use my computer. I spend many hours listening to my "talking books". The Texas State Library Talking Books for the Blind is a wonderful free service I have enjoyed for years. I will lie in bed and listen to books and pass the time and sometimes actually learn something. I still prepare my meals for Saturday and Sunday. Sandwiches are a wonderful invention!

I am developing a sense of contentment each day. It is not easy. I have reduced my excess clothing to a bare minimum, and still have what I need. I wish I had learned to do these things years ago. I wasted so much money on excess clothes and just "stuff". I am thankful for my modest retirement income that meets my needs, but had I been wiser, I could have invested wisely and increased my income to reduce any potential worry about the cost of living, especially the on-going increase in rent. But, my needs are met.

I am learning that God does not hold my past against me. In fact, He has forgotten my past sins and mistakes. I wonder if He is sometimes puzzled why we are so burdened over our past? We don't forgive ourselves, and then try to blame God. This is wrong, stupid and our own ego trying to be greater than God.

I am learning to accept, adjust and embrace my time and my reality. My great teachers are the pets I have had in the past. I love cats and dogs and have enjoyed having both grow up together. The last great teachers were the pets I had in the past. The last 5 years I have not had the companionship of a pet due to apartment regulations. My present apartment has a $300.00 non-refundable pet fee. This is my only negative attitude toward my "nest". I just can't afford to throw that much money away, especially when I have no way to replace it. Now, it is doubtful that I could properly care for a pet due to limited vision. I know I could not handle a dog, but would love a kitten.

Have you noticed that your cat or dog has no problem understanding the value and joy of sleeping? Our world does not give credit to the value of proper sleep. It is always the very last thing we have to do at night. We violate the very rules for restful sleep. The bedroom should be a place of calmness and quietness. It should set the mood and tone for rest. The moment we step into our bedroom it should trigger our senses that this is the place for sleep, rest or sex. But what do we do? We stick a television in the room, or the computer so we can keep our senses excited and the noise level up.

The American home is backward. The smallest bedroom should be the sleeping chamber with calm colors and just the bed. The big master bedroom can be the activity center. But we don't value that. We even violate nature's clock by eating our biggest meal at night rather than at noon. We then wonder why we aren't rested. We are tied to the tempo that we must always be busy, busy and productive. And we wonder why we are a nation of nervous Nellies.

Let me get back to my point. My cat never missed an opportunity to play hard, eat and drink and then take a nap. My dogs lived the same way. They were not concerned with anything else but to love me, be my companion, found their food, go outside or find the litter box and then sleep. The average American does not get a good 8 hours of sleep and the body pays the price. I have now grown away from the use of sleep as an escape. I am trying to find nature's true balance of the ebb and flow of life. I am now ready to get up when I wake and often have a song of praise in my mind. I may or may not take a nap during the day. I have given myself the freedom to do so.

I spend much time resting in bed listening to a book. I was approached by someone about being in bed so much listening to my book. I was asked if I would be happier if I were sitting all day in my recliner? I am resting not hiding. It may not be an exact science, but I feel that after a good rest I can see a little better!

Whether that is true or not, I am learning to reduce my worry time. Please excuse me; it's time for a nap!   I chose to take a nap, join me?

TRUST YOU?
DO I HAVE A CHOICE?

I have a deep appreciation for the old songs of faith. I grew up with the songs that built the inner soul. "Sweet Hour of Prayer", "Rock of Ages", "Kneel at the Cross", "I'll Fly Away", "Faith of our Fathers" "At the Cross" and dozens of other inspired hymns. This is the music I love to play and sing. I enjoy listening to Bill Gaither and his group as they blend their voices.

I haven't been to church much over the past years. I spent 4 years in Laredo, where English is not spoken unless demanded. I was taken to three different churches by well-intentioned people, but my lack of Spanish made the service more of a bust than a blessing. I have attended a couple of churches since returning to Midland, Texas, with less than desirable results.

I don't understand what has happened to worship? It has been reduced to more of a "people-pleasing" frosting. I am aware of the impact of the "New Age" movement on worship. The songs I heard were little gospel ditties and goodie, goodie sound tracks that had no foundation. I heard songs about the nice sky, the singing birds and the nice love that God has. I saw wonderful hymn books catching dust in the pew, while we gawked at a rock-concert type big screen displaying meaningless words. I had never heard of the songs and I couldn't see the words on the screen. I saw the pulpit replaced by a music stand on the floor with the "sermon" more of a "town meeting" discussion. One "church" had completely removed the pulpit. This may be progress but it isn't what touches the soul. Yes, I am old!   I have no appreciation for the TV mega churches. They only promote the ego and bank account of the "star". I was disgusted and sadden when I learned of one "big" TV religious star, who owned 27 houses, each fully staffed in case he or his wife were in that city. The quest of wealth, power and greed has polluted our current preaching generation. How far we have come! Peter said to the man lame, "silver and gold, have we none, but such as have, give we until ye, rise up and walk". We can now brag about how rich the "church" is and nobody is walking. Yes, I know! I am old! I don't miss going to church. I do miss worship with others and not the "wind up monkey band" glee turned on by the modern "leaders of worship".   Yes, I am old...did I mention that? The modern church is failing to teach trust and dependence on God. We are taught to simply "trust yourself." This is actually a half-truth. We can trust the Christ in us after we have allowed Christ to become our guide.

I have to trust others! Well, I really don't. I could make the decision that some others have made. I could become withdrawn, bitter, and hateful, never love again and see the world between my self-pity, inner anger and rage. Yes, I could make that decision and then wonder why I am not only blind, but without anyone to give a hoot?

I have already alluded to the fact that I can no longer do things on my own time schedule. I have to ask and wait for someone else. This covers any aspect of my life. Replacing the milk in the icebox to taking my dirty clothes to the laundry is now a planned event. This is not a bad or negative reality. It depends on my attitude.

Most of us do not like to depend on others. The feeling of being in control is a wide spread source of personal pride. I have heard the ego centered comment, "I don't need anybody". Some people honestly feel that serving others is their highest goal and they don't embrace the concept of accepting help from others. This can come from positive or negative motivation.

I have always been a helper to others. I have been generous and compassionate to the needs of others. This is not my ego speaking. Those who know me will confirm. My "softie" heart has allowed me to be conned, scammed and fleeced by others. I have been unwise but have always felt I would rather be accused of being "too kind" than "hard hearted" when God judges me. I have known and worked for "hard-hearted" people. It is sad that they often have wealth and control, but have no soul worth.

My reducing vision has given me a learning platform even at age 70. I have noticed that my mind and thinking doesn't always match my age and physical reality. I don't feel old! I often have delightful thoughts of doing something for enjoyment; only to discover when

I attempt it, I can't see well enough to do so. My mind still embraces love, romance and the sweetness of companionship. I then discover that I don't have that person to accomplish my "love-thoughts". The simple statement to simply "get out and meet someone" is as a tree falling in the forest. No one hears! I have made some interesting efforts. I have "invested" in on-line dating sites. Chuckle, chuckle. I have attempted to write my "sales pitch" and after the dust settles I have to face my reality. I am 70 years old, nearly blind and have no property and a very modest income. Who am I going to catch? I know what a loving and warm person I am but that is my mind and my desire. The fact is I am becoming an old man.

I remember my attitude when I was invited to attend my high school 50th class reunion. I had not returned to my hometown of Weatherford, Oklahoma since my graduation 50 years ago. This was 2009, I graduated in 1959. My immediate thought was "why do I want to go see all those old people"? I did go and visited all the locations of my growing up years. I discovered that no signs of my ever living there existed. It is a true statement, "You can never go back home". The location of my Dad's bakery was now a pawn shop. The house I grew up in was completed remodeled and even my high school was rebuilt. Life goes on, with or without us sharing in the process.

I have learned the necessity of needing others. I

have a wonderful small group of supporting friends who love and care about me. They are committed to my well-being and pledged to assure I am ok. Just because I have devoted friends does not mean I am their only concern. They have families and jobs and other normal experiences in life. I had to learn not to dump all my needs on just one person, after all, they did not marry me. One has adopted me as "Grandpa" and fills her role as my "granddaughter. I have learned the following excellent rules of living and relationship. I can expect, but not impose expectations! I can respond, but not assign responsibility.

It can be said that faith can be understood in terms of expecting. Positive faith expects the good and negative faith expects the bad. They both work! We are taught to expect God's blessings, His comfort and His peace but we cannot demand when, how and in what manner these will come! I can expect my friends to do and react to me and my needs. I cannot set the limits or time table when it happens. When I make expectations, I set up the formula for disappointment and resentment. I can become resentful and anger because "I waited" "why weren't you here?" I can make myself miserable walking the floor, pulling my hair, (although there is not much left) all because I have placed the burden of meeting my expectations in my time frame. It is the same concept of knowing that I can trust someone but perhaps cannot always depend on them. When I expect, I am open to gratitude rather than annoyance and judgment against you.

The concept of responding without assigning responsibility at first may be seen much the same thing. There is a slight difference. I can respond to the actions of others and enjoy the benefit of their actions. I cannot make them responsible for being the source that feeling full time. Let me explain. I can respond to your kindness that makes me feel good and loved. That is healthy and feeds me with positive results. If I decide that it is your responsibility to ALWAYS make me feel that way, then I place a burden on you that will fail me. It is the same trap when people feel that one person must meet all their needs. We need others in our life that will help us in their unique way. If I make you responsible for my personal feeling of self-worth, then I become a parasite and can kill any good between us.

What is my point? I can trust you without requiring that you meet my standards. I have to trust you if I want to get outside my four walls. I am now trusting total strangers to provide me a hot meal each day. I have to trust someone to deliver that meal every day, rain, shine, snow or storm. What I have to guard against is having no ability for the unexpected. I am in trouble if I cannot survive if a meal does not arrive. I can call someone else or fix a simple bowl of cereal. I can do that without my world crashing over one meal.

Ah, now I can apply that same concept to my life. I can expect to meet the demands of each day. I wake up each morning with the inner thought of whether my vision will be less today than yesterday. No, this is not negative confession. This is a statement of reality. I can get very sad if I dwell on the fact of my dimming vision. I can look back and remember when I could see across my room, when I could see inside in icebox, when I could see the temperature on the stove knobs or when I could see water boiling for whatever food I was cooking. Yes, I can see the decline in my vision. I see only a faint image in my mirror as I shave and brush my teeth. I have learned to push the toothpaste into my mouth since I cannot see the toothbrush. This is reality but it does not have to control me. I can control my limitations as they appear. This is not Pollyanna but the awareness that I can make the decision to sink into despair, or rise to the situation. The responsibility for my personal well-being has to be mine. There is some truth is the statement, "Laugh and the world laughs with you, cry and you cry alone". I must learn that I am not a blind man yet, but is a man who is becoming blind. I cannot allow my limitation to become my identity. This is not denial but it is a healthy embrace.

I cannot describe the awful pain, pain and panic that I can feel at times. When I look at my clothes in the closet I can no longer tell what colors go together. My mind wants to do common things that I can no longer do. The inner isolation and the fear and dread of facing tomorrow is like a flood of mud covering you. I have to ask someone what is in my freezer, what is in the cans on my pantry? This is not fun. It is not fair. I did not ask for it. So, what is the point? I have learned to make my woe verbal in prayer. I am learning to understand that I want to accept God's control in my life, but at the same time I don't want to. I can understand Jesus praying, "If it be possible, let this cup pass from me". I pray the same prayer and then ask forgiveness for my fear and lack of faith. God is faithful but my friends can grow tired of my constant whining and "woe is me" attitude. They are not God and they have no control over my world. They can help me as I embrace my world. They can be my support and show me love and allow me to share with them, but my cross is mine. I cannot push my friends under my cross and hope to walk away.

I am learning to trust that I will have the vision needed for today. That is all I can expect and use. The senseless fear of the future and the life draining guilt of the past serve no purpose. We have today. We have now. When I do look back and review mistakes, I have to remind myself that I made decisions based on who and what I was at that point. I cannot change, amend or cancel that fact.

I can trust and obey what I know now. I can continue to do and enjoy what is possible. As things vanish it will be my choice to find a replacement. I am having more good days than bad. I am slowly hearing the choir in my soul starting to sing again. I find myself with tearful appreciation for my blessings rather than angry rage over what has been lost.

I am having to practice what I preached. God made no attempt to explain Himself. He does not ask us to understand Him or His ways. He asks us to trust and obey Him. Understanding comes AFTER obedience. Trust and obey. Isn't it amazing how simple yet so hard? It is sad that we have made God so complex and His Way so obscure by our religious nonsense. Forget the rules and meet the rule-giver!

IF YOU TOUCH ME...
I'LL FIND MY WAY!

I am daily addressing the awareness of how important vision is. It is true that any limiting problem has an impact. The loss of vision is no greater than the person who can no longer hear or walk. The problem that affects you is the one you are most concerned with. That being true, let me affirm that each of us with a "limit" probably would not want to trade with someone else. We each carry our own bag of rocks in life. The "value" of each 'bag of rocks" is determined by how and what we learn in dealing with our reality! I have mentioned before that the thought of being vision-impaired had never closed my mind. I never thought I would face my "golden years" living alone; never mind being almost blind!

My task now is to be honest. I can think too much, complain too much and in general allow my blindness to destroy my world. This is probably the easy road to take. I have struggled over the years and have slowly gained insight that allows me to experience some joy in living again. I can now look back and realize how much time we waste in efforts that are not worthwhile. I have realized that I have been a victim of wrong goals and accomplishments. Thanks to the nature of God, He forgives and forgets. It is to our discredit that we fight

forgetting and forgiving.

The ability to trust is optional in our daily living. I have heard the whine of those who have been hurt, "I will never trust again". "Don't let anyone get a leg up on you". These are the expressions of those who refuse to embrace life and love. They allow grief, greed, anger and self-centeredness cover their world. These people are to be avoided but prayed for. They offer no value to others. It is sadly true that many of these people are "successful" in terms of wealth and control, but they are victims that refuse help. They generally feel that know more than others and more than God. They are dangerous people! The lessons of trust and humility are signs of weakness in their estimation.

I have commented on the reality of losing independence in the case of vision loss. The argument can be made that this is the single greatest rock to carry. The vision-impaired person quickly learns that they must depend on others for many situations. The quick trip to the corner store is no longer an option. The jump in the car to go for a loaf of bread is but a memory. The accomplishments of life are now determined by the time table and interest of a third party. This can be an exercise in frustration or a lesson in gracious waiting. You learn to adjust to "I forgot" or "I was too busy" and not take it as a personal rejection. I would be lying if I did not confess that I miss my freedom. I have to be careful just walking to the mail shack in my apartment complex. I have gotten lost a couple of times by going too early in the day and the glare was too great.

One of my enjoyments is going out to eat or to shop. I have always needed some help due to the glare of bright lights and the boring over use of the color white in stores. While living in Laredo, Texas, I had a couple who would take me places and then go off and leave me! They didn't understand my need for "touch". That need has gotten greater over the past 2 years. I cannot explain the panic and terror that can cover you with you cannot see where you are going. The lack of vision curtails your coordination and sense of balance. Why? I don't know…I just know how it affects me!

I do fairly well in my apartment as it is organized and the lack of vision is less damaging. I wish my vision would continue without becoming less; but the reality is different. I can notice the difference monthly. So be it!

What I now know is that I am totally dependent on my guide in any out-door situation. I have a special 'guide-girl" who has been the joy of my life for over 10 years. She is my sweetheart and the daughter I wish I had. She has the ability to make me secure in any situation. We go out monthly and she never allows me to be "lost".

The sense of touch is necessary for my security. Yes, I have met people who have learned to avoid touch. They have forsaken the natural desire to be touch as expressed in babyhood. These people have lost a lot and could not be of any help to me. I need the security of someone touching me and leading me if I am out-doors or in a store. I cannot express how scary it is to suddenly be alone, unable to see and not know where you are or what is in front of you. The touch of a hand becomes a healing factor and the world becomes friendly again. Yes, I need you to touch and direct me. I had a former friend who kept pointing at things and telling me to go or look where he was pointing. I had to tell me, like man, I can't see where you are pointing. You have to lead me. He never got the message and is no longer a part of my world. That was his choice.

What's my point? I have learned the sweetness and security of the touch of a friend. I have a greater appreciation of the old Gospel song, "The Touch of the Master's Hand"…or maybe it is a poem? You look it up. I can now better relate to the kindness and love that the touch of God gives when we surrender to it. Yes, I said surrender. We like to be our own boss and the captain of our own ship. All that is nonsense! I had to learn to surrender to the touch of an earthly guide the hard way. I now appreciate the touch of Jesus in a deeper way and I find His touch in your touch. If you are going to lead me, you have to touch me!

IF I CAN'T SEE YOU ANYMORE, WILL YOU GO AWAY?

It is common for older people to look back in time. The "good old days" are often spoken on in terms of endearment. A common practice is to make the past smoother or kinder than the actual reality. I am not exempt from the backward review and rehashing of events. I don't know if this is good or bad; but I know it is a common usage of time. I am learning to allow these backward trips to become lessons learned and forgiveness granted; both to myself and others.

Have you reviewed the friends that passed by your doorstep? It is said that the human body replaces itself every 7 years in body cell growth. I wonder how often we exchange our group of friends. We have childhood friends who were "best buddies" and they become memories as we grow up, move away or have a fight and the association is over. We have business friends that come and go over the years. It takes some maturity to begin to understand that people play a role in our life and not always the same one. The Bible teaches the concept of "seasons". There is a time to laugh, a time to cry, a time to plant and a time to harvest. This is part of the process of living. We sometimes drive people away from us by our stubborn opinions or anger or just because we get tired of that person. People will be drawn to us and then withdraw from us, they may or may not know why.

I have learned the value of friendship in a very personal way over the last 10 years. The truth is I must have a few friends to survive. I think this is true for everyone; but many may never embrace that understanding. It has been said, but I don't remember who said, that if you have 2 or 3 friends you are blessed. A friend is a person who accepts you with no plans to change you. This should be the pattern for marriage, but often we marry with the thought we can change the other person.

I have learned to understand why people stop being your friend. This does not make it less stressful, but it does reduce the need to be angry at yourself or the other person. I have talked about how people handle grief in their own way. This understanding has helped me understand some loss I have had in terms of personal friendship. I have had the "book learning" that people are uncomfortable around "disabled" people. I saw this in action during my career as a nursing home administrator. One of the major complaints of the elderly in a nursing home is that "no one touches me anymore" or "no one talks to me anymore". The person in the wheelchair is aware that they always have to look up to talk with someone. Our society does not prepare us to embrace the old or the disabled. I have seen men and women become awkward and ill at ease around the disabled and elderly. I have had to laugh to myself as people react to me as a "blind" person by talking louder. I experienced this during travel on airlines. I had to tell one person that I was blind but not deaf. When you understand the lack of training given to the general population on how to deal with the disabled, you can accept and forgive the actions of people who hurt you, without intent.

I have lost a few long term friends since losing my vision. This was a painful and depressing experience for a long time. I clearly understood that the Bible teaches that we are never alone; however, there are those times when you really need flesh and blood companions. The biggest loss involved a friendship of almost 25 years. This covered work, social and spiritual involvement and a "forever" bonding. I felt the love and support strongly and learned to depend on it. The relationship crashed as I became less and less capable to function due to my dimming vision. I was no longer as strong or assertive as an individual. I then realized that my friends were not able to handle my loss of independence. They could not deal with watching me "waste" away as a strong person. It could be said that their love could not stand to watch me slip into helpless dependence on others. So they abandoned me. I have seen this in other situations and understand that it is a reality and not a fault or defect. I now value those who care and love me regardless of my condition. I must allow the freedom of going or staying in my world by those who walk by me. I am blessed with a safety net to sustain me. I can now bless those who became a part of my past and not squeeze to death those who remain.

When I reach out for you, I hope you will always be there; but if you have to leave, I will be thankful for the time we had. You don't have to sign a contract with me. I will always expect your love; but will not put expectations of how that love must be displayed. My goal is to be a good friend to those in my world. You are most welcome!

Truth or Fiction?
I don't care! I think I can see better!

I never know when I wake up how my vision is going to be for the day! I have mentioned that my ability to see is slowly becoming dimmer. This is the nature of the eye defect I have. I have now had almost 10 years of history dealing with this problem. I am learning daily. Some days I learn with joy and delight and other days it is like scraping your fingernails over a blackboard. I have often stated that it is much easier to "preach" than "to live" the various teachings of the Bible. It is the shadows that produce the contrast in any picture. The hard times make it possible to recognize the good times. This isn't rocket science!

I have relearned the solid relationship between what we think and how we feel or act. This can be called "positive thinking", "metaphysical teachings" or simply the teaching of the Bible; *"as a man thinketh in his heart, so is he."* The Bible also teaches that "from the abundance of the heart, man speaks". Like it or not, the power of the mind is creative in the reality of our living. The Theropon Institute, where I was licensed as a "Belief Therapist", teaches that we behave according to what we believe. This is the psychological model of the Therapon Therapist.

What we keep in our thoughts will dictate the direction of our day. Have you noticed that after you buy a red car how many red cars you notice? It is a matter of what we expect and look for. The Bible teaches that we should 'guard" our thinking.   If I understand the relationship between my thought life and the reality of my world, I start to understand how I can become active in the quality of life. If I become a blind person, then my whole world revolves around blindness. If I am a person who is blind, then I allow all the other aspects of who I am to continue to grow.

I have noticed, and this is strictly personal, that when I dwell on my blindness I can expect panic, fear and loss of pleasure to quickly invade my day. This I have noticed in a very active way. I have learned that people are not long interested in your "blindness" but will continue to be attracted to "who" you are and were. I can control that. I am talking about the ease of having a "pity party" and singing the "woe is me" song. The task is to continue to active in the process of life and living. The rub comes as you decline in the ability to do those things that kept you busy. I used to love to read. I can't read well enough to enjoy it anymore. It is a struggle just for me to write a check and that will soon vanish. I enjoyed cooking and I have already explain how that is quickly a part of my history. I enjoyed watching movies and television but that is slowly blurring away. I have long enjoyed making coffee coasters, pencil holders and desk top box collectors out of plastic weave and now, you guessed it. The threading of Bible needle is almost gone with the Dodo bird. I can still enjoy playing computer games, especially Book Worm. It uses big letters but I can see the ending at the end of the tunnel. That leaves me with my enjoyment of listening to "talking books" which I do enjoy. That leaves me with the pleasure of talking.

What do I do? I can spend all my time in the past and cry over the losses, or I can put energy into what I can still do. I can still be taken out to eat without embarrassing myself or others. That may change in time. I do enjoy listening to my books and I can always talk. The problem with talking is that you need a listener. I have a small circle of supporters who will come at the drop of a pin if I have a need but each does have a personal life and family. I know they are all just a phone call always but cannot make me the "center" of their world. Ah, the lack of a wife. I have commented on the blessing of "Meals on Wheels". I finally asked for additional help from the Midland Community Services in the form of their program "Senior Companion program. This is a service of volunteers who make regular visits to those who are "homebound. They can provide light housekeeping, light cooking, run errands and someone just to visit.

I am assigned a 76 year old gentleman, Stan. He comes from 11:00 to 2:00 p.m. Monday thru Friday and we visit. I would have liked to have had a "Susan" but the service isn't a "dating service!" I have to express my delight in having someone to share the day with. We are a perfect pair as he is content to talk, to watch television news or simply to visit. There are times when we 'cat-nap", me on the sofa and he on the love -seat. It is very comfortable and I look forward our "un-pressured" time. This helps keep me from thinking about my "pity party" very much. What's my point? The less time we dwell on our personal self, and allow other interests to take our time, the less time we have for gloom, doom and despair. It is our choice!

I have good days and I have bad days! So what else is new? I want to be very clear that I truly believe that the Good Lord is in control at all times. This knowledge does not prevent me from having my doubts and fears. I have learned that the God I serve isn't dethroned just because I have a few fears or get panic. God does not ask me to "lie" about how I feel. How many times a "good" Christian will comment, "You shouldn't feel that way". That is like telling someone who falls out of a chair they shouldn't hit the floor! Feelings are not good or bad, they just ARE what they are! Feelings are reality. The test is HOW we deal with the feelings. This is where our faith is tested and grows or is allowed to die for lack of use. *"The trying of your faith worketh patience."* I don't enjoy that process, but that does not change the reality. I understand the power of the mind over the body. I have had some experiences that I truly cannot fully explain but have to admit their reality. I have explained that I tend to sleep a lot and 'rest. I spend time listening to my books while still resting in bed. I could rest in my rocking chair but I don't see the difference it sitting up or resting down. During weekends I often spend most of the time listening in bed. I have noticed that often after much rest I have a better vision the next day! I do understand that sleep is a natural healer of the body. This may be just "in my head" but it seems to follow a pattern.

I have explained that I take no medicine for any health problems. I do take herbs as Saw Palmetto, St. John's Wort, Vitamin A and a combination formulated to help vision. I recently added Ginko Biloba after learning it helped blood circulation and might help the health of the eyes. Maybe they are helping? Who knows, but I will take what comes.

My next experience is a puzzle and could upset some of my good "Baptist" friends. I was raised in the Assemblies of God church. It can be said that they are the "mother church" of the Pentecostal group. Yes, I grew up with a very strict and fundamental view of the Bible. I have had that background mocked and made fun of by those of small minds. I have indicated that as a part of my spiritual walk I saw the problems of the "church" and expanded my view of the Kingdom. I have an appreciation of my past without having to be enslaved to it.

I have taught that drinking beer or wine or any alcoholic drink would bring the immediate wrath of almighty God. I preached this with vigor and energy. I even endorsed the notion that Jesus must have had stock in Welsh's Grape Juice when he turned the water into wine. The facts do not support that theory. My apologies to my Baptist friends. No I don't want any letters; I just learned that moderation was taught by the Bible. I do not remember how or when I had my first drink of beer and wine. This will shock a few? There was a time after my divorce that I cradled the bottle often.

I had a good Congregational Minister who knew my background and knew that I would 'adjust back" in time. He was my bumper guard to help me during some hard times. I did mellow out and put my faith and trust in God back in place at the center of my world. I also had a different understanding of social drinking. The real freedom is to be able to NOT drink or TO drink, not just a fear or guilt trip about drinking. No you don't have to agree, this is my story. I have also learned that everyone does not have to walk the same path I walk. I believe we all have to start at the Cross and the Blood saving grace, but God leads us and not the church. My thoughts. What's my point? I have explained that over the past years I have had my deep shadows of depression, fear and panic. Sometimes I would drink 3 or 4 beers in the evening. Believe it or not, I started to notice that the day after these days I would see a little better. I explained this to one of my close friends who told me that "maybe I should be a drunk with good vision" as he laughed with me. I have paid attention and have discovered that I often see better the next day after my beers! No, I don't know why and I am not going to drown each day in cheap beer, but truth or fiction…I have had better vision days. So perhaps I will have wine with my "meals on wheels"?

IT'S A SMALL, SMALL WORLD, AFTER ALL!

I started this section at 4 a.m. on Friday morning. I couldn't sleep, which is often the case. I have learned to finally just get up and "do" something. One of my past times is to make coffee coasters out of plastic canvass. I give them away when I encounter people. It makes the time go faster and I can listen to a book or music while being creative.

I have discovered that I spend more time "living" in my mind. Since I cannot longer see well enough to enjoy it, I spend much time in thought and reliving past events. This may not be very unusual for the old? I don't know, but it brings me some pleasure and sometimes some sadness.

I have had a good life, not a perfect life, not a life without pain and heart ache and certainly not with riches; but it has been a good one. God has a plan for each of us, and if we understand Him, He has more than just one. We are free agents and can make choices. We can choose to avoid God's plan and go our own way. He is then able to make our rebellion to "work together for good". I look back and accept that I side stepped God's perfect will for me; but discovered His permissive will and He covered me anyway. Moses retained the favor of God after Moses disobeyed and HIT the rock for water, rather than SPEAKING to it, but he was denied the opportunity to enter the "Promised Land" due to his disobedience. I have come to the conclusion that we are forgiven by God but still have to deal with the harvest or the results of our actions.

I have enjoyed many roles in my life. I learned the hard lesson that God is not found inside ANY one church nor does he favor any church label. The power of the Bible has been so weaken by our "religion" that even God would not claim ownership to what we try to force people to believe. My last experience with the "organized" church forced me to see and feel the wrath of the corruption in church politics. This pushed me into all of the "tent-making" jobs mentioned. I understand Paul the tent-maker very well.

I look back on these years and shake my head. Where did the time go? I can clearly see, to my satisfaction, the guiding hand of the Lord, even when I was not "living my beliefs". Please understand that I am not suggesting that we spend a lot of time looking back. We cannot change the past and can only learn from it. Once the learning is embraced, there is little purpose to revisit the event but build for the future.

My childhood was blessed and full of God's grace. I was adopted by two hand-picked parents to guide my life. My Godly mother taught me to love God and my gentle Dad taught me to be kind and accept people as they are. If things go well, I will explore my unique childhood in another book. But let it be understood that my parents were selected by a loving God to give me a solid foundation in love and grace. I had to grow into full understanding the hard way.

My personal life was not a testimony to my faithfulness to God's plan. That may or may not be the subject of another book. Some things are best learned and kept private! Let me simply state that at this point in my life, age may or may not be the subject of another book. Let me simply state that at this point in my life, at age 70, living alone and almost totally blind, I can accept that my decisions in the past made the path possible to my present situation. I married out of the will of God and followed my own personal goals and ambitions.

It is a fact that I have been forgiven for my past errors, but the planted seeds did produce a harvest. God is a God of grace and he does not remember my mistakes anymore and He gives me His support as I manage the "harvest". I, like, Moses, may not be able to have the "promised land" of a mate again, but God cannot be blamed for the results of seed planted.

I review all my past and recognize that it is a small world. I remember hearing that happy song in Orlando, Florida, many years ago while visiting Disney World. I was with a group of friends and we were planning to ride the roller coaster. The theme music was, of course, "It's a small, small world". The girl I was with was so excited and told me, "I love the roller coaster and I get so excited

I sometimes wet my pants". I quickly suggested that she sit in front of my seat. I have always been a gentleman!

I understand the small world even better as a blind person. When you cannot see, you don't move around as much and your activities are limited. I am learning to enjoy the vigor of my mind and to embrace my blessings. I am understanding more each day the teachings that we *are to lean not to your own understanding, but in all thy ways acknowledge Me and I will direct thy paths.*" I wake up with a prayer and praise almost daily with the understanding that my small world is full of grace and love from God. I wish I had a few more "flesh and blood" friends, but God knows that also. I miss the companion of a pet, a kitten at this point, as I could not 'walk a dog" in the apartment. It's a small world, but it is large enough for my needs. I still have dreams and hopes. I hope to "fall in love" again! Now, if you would just lead me a cliff?

I look back on these years and shake my head. Where did the time go? I can clearly see, to my satisfaction, the guiding hand of the Lord, even when I was not "living my beliefs." Please understand that I am not suggesting that we spend a lot of time looking back. We cannot change the past and can only learn from it. Once the learning is embraced, there is little purpose to revisit the event but build for the future.

My childhood was blessed and full of God's grace. I was adopted by two hand-picked parents to guide my life. My Godly mother taught me to love God and my gentle Dad taught me to be kind and accept people as they are. If things go well, I will explore my unique childhood in another book. But let it be understood that my parents were selected by a loving God to give me a solid foundation in love and grace. I had to grow into full understanding the hard way.

Let me simply state that at this point in my life, at age 70, living alone and almost totally blind was never a part of my thought process. I can accept that my decisions in the past made the path possible to my present situation. I married out of the Will of God and followed my own personal goals and ambitions.

I understand the small world even better as a blind person. When you cannot see, you don't move around as much and your activities are limited. I am learning to enjoy the vigor of my mind and to embrace my blessings. I am understanding more each day the teachings that we *are to lean not to your own understanding, but in all thy ways acknowledge Me and I will direct thy paths.*" I wake up with a prayer and praise almost daily with the understanding that my small world is full of grace and love from God. I wish I had a few more "flesh and blood" friends, but God knows that also. I miss the companion of a pet, a kitten at this point, as I could not 'walk a dog" in the apartment. It's a small world, but it is large enough for my needs. I still have dreams and hopes.

Meet Your Author

Fred Don Cullens

Fred Cullens is a retired Minister and Nursing Home Administrator. He lives in Arlington, Texas with his girlfriend, Bronx, a four pawed tortoise shell cat, and his close friend who cooks and shops for him and Bronx.